Private Vocational Schools and Their Students:

LIMITED OBJECTIVES
UNLIMITED OPPORTUNITIES

by

A. Harvey Belitsky

THE W. E. UPJOHN INSTITUTE
FOR EMPLOYMENT RESEARCH

SCHENKMAN PUBLISHING COMPANY, INC.
CAMBRIDGE, MASSACHUSETTS

Contents

Appendixes

To HELEN

Preface

Nations at war, even "peaceful" wars, often discover hidden strengths which are apt to be called "secret weapons." With the war on poverty, we have discovered the value of institutions and people often ignored; these include private business firms as well as neighborhood residents working for local "poverty" programs.

The value of another one of these private institutions — the proprietary vocational school — is the principal subject of this book.

As with most contractual arrangements, a basic mutuality of interest obtains among profit-seeking schools and their students. The schools, responding to the incentives normally associated with the production of services and goods, provide their students with a training that is highly practical and job-oriented. This training per se serves as an incentive to many students — including the disadvantaged — who are likely to be motivated by instruction that has a direct connection with the ultimate requirements of a job.

The study shows that the schools have yet to be fully exploited under various training programs. This is the case despite the schools' demonstrated capacities to serve severely disadvantaged people under a variety of government programs. For instance, over several decades most, if not all, state Vocational Rehabilitation agencies have contracted with these private schools for training of many of their clients.

America has been cited for its commitment to equality of educational opportunity and the fullest personal development by all members of the labor force. It follows that scarce training resources should be fully employed. This nation need not await sporadic discovery and identification of its people and institutions as "secret weapons."

Acknowledgments

I am grateful to The Ford Foundation which financed the research for this study over a 15-month period and to Mr. Marvin J. Feldman of the Foundation who encouraged me during each stage of the work.

Dr. Herbert E. Striner of The Upjohn Institute suggested the basic idea of this book and provided advice throughout the study and critical comments on drafts of the manuscript. I am also indebted to other colleagues at the Institute. Dr. Irving H. Siegel recommended numerous excellent revisions of an early version of the book. Dr. Joseph E. Morton advised me regarding the most effective statistical application

Acknowledgments

of the often limited data. At the outset of the study I was aided by
the clear-sighted views of Dr. Harold T. Smith, an educator with several decades of experience as a university professor and administrator
and as a researcher at The Upjohn Institute.

Dr. Harold S. Sloan, President of the Institute for Instructional Improvement graciously shared with me his file of materials acquired
while examining private "specialty" schools. Kenneth B. Hoyt, Professor
of Education at the University of Iowa, provided me with several important insights into the schools' operations and he was exceptionally
kind in offering me the use of much of the data collected under his
Specialty Oriented Student Research Program. Chapter 9 is based
upon these materials, and Dr. William D. Griffith, now with the University of Missouri in St. Louis, secured the computerized results analyzed there. Dr. Regis Walther of the George Washington University
Social Research Group prepared the attitudinal questions administered
to students at RCA Institutes, Inc., in New York City, arranged for the
processing of the data and assisted in analyzing the results.

I am greatly indebted to many representatives of the private schools
and their associations. In particular, I thank William Goddard, Executive Director of the National Association of Trade and Technical
Schools, for cheerfully sharing his abundant experience and knowledge
and for introducing me to scores of exceptionally cooperative school
owners. I also acknowledge the generous help of Richard A. Fulton,
Executive Director of the United Business Schools Association, and
Eugene W. Davis, Assistant Executive Director of the Association; and
N. Michael Terzian, Dean of Administration at RCA Institutes, Inc.

As a consultant, Dr. Harriet A. Mintz's contributions included the
effective organization of much of the data for statistical interpreta-
tion. Miss June Shmelzer, also a consultant, prepared some of the
questions and the final format of the questionnaire appearing in Appendix II. Miss Rosanne Burch carefully assembled and recorded the
materials associated with a national survey of the schools. Mrs. Anne
Williams patiently and expertly typed two versions of the manuscript,
prepared the index and suggested numerous editorial improvements.
Finally, my wife Helen was of foremost help and support to me in
many ways, including the editing of the manuscript.

This lengthy yet still incomplete list of acknowledgments reflects in
part the largely unexplored state of the subject of the book. Nevertheless the errors and shortcomings in the book are naturally only mine.

A. Harvey Belitsky

Washington, D.C.
March, 1969

CHAPTER 1

Purpose

This study was undertaken primarily to determine how (or even whether) private vocational schools could be widely utilized in the training of "disadvantaged" persons. Early reading disclosed, however, that even less is known about these frequently ignored schools and their students than about the disadvantaged whom such schools might serve. Equally important, and even astounding, many of the schools have been training persons with various disabilities for several decades.

The study's original purpose remains a primary one, but attention will also be focused upon the workings of private vocational schools. This broader perspective is desirable for at least estimating the number, diversity, and quality of training opportunities available in such schools.

The limited awareness of the potential contributions by the private vocational schools also happens to be the condition that has often plagued "disadvantaged" persons. Society has been moving to remedy many persons' handicaps; the identification, training and employment of the disadvantaged have become important and widely-heralded concerns in recent years.

On the other hand, the schools remain quite unknown — and profitable. A natural question arises: How can private vocational schools exist and even flourish in spite of 1) meager recognition and, at times, opposition to their operations; and 2) the competition of public vocational schools and industry training programs?

The answer is quite simple: Most private schools are profit-making, and like any privately sold good or service, *effective demand* — in this case, for training — must exist at a level that meets all costs and also yields profits. The earning of profits is an indication either that the types of training offered in such schools are unavailable in public schools or elsewhere, or that the students and their advisers (usually parents or friends and, at times, a government agency) consider the private schools' resources superior.

The schools and their students have enunciated an objective of full-time employment following completion of specific occupational training courses. Naturally, the practical requirements of prospective employers affect the contents of every course.

Although general patterns of operation are discernible within the private schools, a number of *exceptional* practices were also found. This diversity should not be too surprising to economists. The private school owner or administrator bears some resemblance to the entrepreneurs and executives in most private business ventures. Therefore, when necessary, the individual needs of students and employers have been accommodated.

Limited Objectives,
Unlimited Opportunities

The paradox emphasized in this book's title deserves explanation. The schools offer a great variety of courses or programs that prepare for direct employment. Courses are "limited" to specific occupational training in scores of fields, including air conditioning, automobile repair, drafting, electronic technology, medical assisting, photography, welding, and such untraditional fields as baseball umpiring and horseshoeing. Despite (or perhaps because of) their specialized or "limited" objectives there are thousands of such schools; and as a group the schools appear to have unlimited opportunity for growth.

A designation like "limited objectives" can have its own limitations. It may have little relevance for many persons of low aptitudes or low aspirations — including high school dropouts who lack any employment experience or persons working for long periods on jobs which leave much of their potential untapped. The job skills learned in private vocational schools (far from being limiting or limited) can be an effective and time-saving substitute for on-the-job training, which may in any case be unavailable in some occupations, or at least to young persons who have no employment experience. The graduates of these schools are placed in positions which may offer room for advancement through either internal promotions or further institutional training and education on a part-time basis. There are other graduates of private schools who may reach their occupational peaks immediately following completion of training through placement in occupations related to their training. Therefore the concept of training for limited objectives is a highly relative one.

Educators, guidance counselors and manpower specialists may oppose training for limited objectives because they consider such training inferior to broader or more generalized education. Although general education may be more appropriate for the purpose of making lifetime occupational adjustments, this is only true for certain persons.

The argument may have little meaning for persons who can be stimulated only by training which is both job-related and provides basic education directly relevant to the occupational training.

Private Vocational Schools and the Disadvantaged

This book shows some of the mutual interests of private vocational schools and disadvantaged persons.[1]

Chapters 2–4 are concerned with the schools. Chapter 2 attempts to define the important social role that private vocational schools can play through the variety of vocational training they provide for a multitude of people. Chapter 3 describes the advantages to students and employers that derive from the impressive flexibility of the schools' operations. The progress toward meaningful evaluation of the schools through voluntary accreditation is discussed in Chapter 4.

Chapters 5 and 6 are concerned with instruction. Chapter 5 highlights aspects of instruction which have proven successful in motivating and training persons with diverse interests and capacities — ranging from the severely disadvantaged enrolled in a laundry helper course to highly talented individuals enrolled in a demanding two-year course for engineering technicians. As seen in Chapter 6, the varied demands upon instructors include individual teaching and even student counseling.

Chapters 7–9 are devoted to the characteristics, needs and performance of students attending private vocational schools. Chapter 7 demonstrates that the schools could accommodate many more trainees who are not high school graduates. It also becomes evident that financial need is the prime reason for students' failure to complete their courses. Chapter 8 presents data on student responses to proposed financial aid programs. Chapter 9 attempts to ascertain how school dropouts perform in competition with other students attending private vocational schools.

The final two chapters illustrate the potential for expanding the

[1] No attempt is made to formulate a comprehensive definition of the "disadvantaged"; there are surely multiple causes, including personal, educational, cultural and financial handicaps. Moreover, a major group among the "disadvantaged" is comprised of young persons from middle income families who are enrolled in high school programs they find uninteresting for lack of specific occupational objective.

It is also difficult to define the schools precisely, but they are distinguishable by being private (in contrast to governmental) and by their concern with training for explicitly stated occupational objectives, rather than the academic degree awarded by most colleges and universities. Some characteristics of the major occupational categories of private vocational schools are considered in Chapter 2.

training of disadvantaged persons through existing and new government programs. Recommendations for joint public-private training programs and financial grants to students enrolled in private vocational schools would benefit the disadvantaged as well as other student groups.

CHAPTER 2

Social Role of Private Vocational Schools

"Fortunately for us, we [the private vocational schools] have identified our particular goals and know what excellence is in terms of these goals, and we have established our educational program (learning through doing) in order to produce these results . . ."
— CHARLES MATHIS, Director,
Eastern School for
Physicians' Aides,
New York, New York

Private vocational schools have been generally ignored — except by students attending the schools and by employers who have hired their graduates.[1] This non-recognition has somewhat limited the growth of the profit-seeking schools; and it could only be highly speculative to estimate the extent to which this has stimulated the schools' administrators to develop distinctive courses and student bodies. However, the following chapter does present the private schools as frequent innovators. As a further effect of this general disregard, proprietary schools and their programs have assumed virtually mythical proportions in the public mind. Myths are necessarily pervaded with unknowns, and this certainly characterizes the private vocational schools.

The training objectives of the private schools — although stated very explicitly by the schools — are not generally known; little is known even about the number of schools and their students. It therefore follows that even less is known about the diverse courses of instruction that are offered.

This chapter is mainly concerned with attempting to provide reasons for the persistence of these "unknowns." Some qualified data are then offered on the sizable numbers of schools, students and types of courses.

[1] Another obviously interested group has been the school owners, whose assets are estimated at $1 billion. See "The Teaching Business," *Barron's*, April 8, 1968, p. 11.

The Myth of "Equal" Educational Opportunity

The lack of basic facts regarding vocational education applies to the public as well as to the private schools. There are admittedly substantial challenges even to the compilation of a directory of courses offered nationally in public vocational schools. They involve the need to classify schools and courses that are often neither uniform nor easy to separate from general education programs. Not until 1968, therefore, was a census of the public vocational schools and their major program areas (e.g., agriculture, trades and industry, and office occupations) made available.[2]

But other factors besides the great diversity in local vocational school courses account for the lack of a regularly published census. After all, for decades censuses of a variety of private business and industrial enterprises have been conducted and published by the U. S. Department of Commerce. The U. S. Office of Education, nonprofit organizations and university researchers have analyzed programs and written extensively on college preparatory or general educational programs in high schools. It may be understandable that efforts have been focused upon those schools whose students comprise the greatest proportion of the high school population. At the same time, public vocational education has received less than its fair share of attention from scholars and researchers.

The minor interest in vocational education simply reflects its low esteem compared with college preparatory programs. Middle-class parents, according to Dr. James B. Conant and others, are responsible for much of the denigration of vocational education. Such parents often merely ignore signs that their children lack interest in a college preparatory program; or they may actively try to make their children see what is "best" for them — i.e., college.

Children in low-income families are even more likely to be misguided (or not guided at all) regarding their optimal educational opportunities. Several researchers have observed:

> Concern of parents for basic necessities of life, low level of educational development of the parents, frequent absence of male parents, lack of interaction between children and adults all conspire to reduce stimulation, language development and intellectual development of such children.[3]

[2] See Center for Studies in Vocational and Technical Education, *Directory of Vocational Education Programs* 1966 (Madison: University of Wisconsin, 1968).

[3] Benjamin S. Bloom, Allison Davis, and Robert Hess, *Compensatory Education for Cultural Deprivation* (New York: Holt, Rinehart and Winston, 1965),

For all of these reasons, students who are reared by poor parents tend to be under-represented in college preparatory programs; neither do they receive careful parental guidance with respect to vocational education.

As an additional handicap to the effective development of vocational education, most school counselors (as shown in Chapter 6) devote only a small share of their efforts to vocational students; and they are, moreover, often inadequately informed on how to counsel such students on future training and employment opportunities. Again, the counselors' lack of interest in this area is an index to more generally held views, which are ultimately expressed through sparing outlays for vocational education.

All of this is startling in view of the fact that 75 percent of America's young people, after all, do *not* graduate from a 4-year college or university.[4] It must be inferred, therefore, that the heavy emphasis upon college preparatory programs in the high schools is misguided.

Ironically, the comparative neglect of vocational education is inconsistent with the laudable social goal of equal educational opportunity. That is, wide variations in both student capabilities and interests are either ignored or given insufficient account. The almost single-minded dedication to maximum enrollment in college preparatory programs has the effect of concealing such realities as: 1) the relatively small number of students matriculated in colleges and universities; and 2) the considerably smaller number actually earning degrees. Dr. John W. Gardner has keenly stressed some central errors in our "philosophy" of education:

> The crowding in our colleges is less regrettable than the confusion in our values. *Human dignity and worth should be assessed only in terms of those qualities of mind and spirit that are within the reach of every human being.*[5]

In short, the goal of equal educational opportunity — as it has been pursued thus far — is virtually a public myth, and besides, unattainable and even illiberal. The goal must be pursued in concert with "excellence" at all levels of study and work. Once again, Dr. Gardner is extremely perceptive:

reported by Elinor F. McCloskey, *Urban Disadvantaged Pupils*, A Synthesis of 99 Research Reports (Portland, Oregon: Northwest Regional Educational Laboratory, 1967), pp. 16–17.

[4] J. Kenneth Little, "The Occupations of Non-College Youth," *American Educational Research Journal*, Vol. 4, No. 2 (March 1967), p. 147.

[5] John W. Gardner, *Excellence* (New York: Harper & Row, 1961), p. 81.

A conception which embraces many kinds of excellence at many levels is the only one which fully accords with the richly varied potentialities of mankind; it is the only one which will permit high morale throughout the society.[6]

In view of the unrealistic emphasis upon college preparatory programs, it is quite natural that many public school systems have hardly recognized the existence of private vocational schools. The private schools have been disregarded because of their irrelevance to the myth of "equal" educational opportunity that has been fashioned. However, even without the myth, some school systems or professional associations may simply fear the competition of the proprietary schools.

There may also be a conviction that proprietary schools are unsavory per se; and therefore the vocational training offered in profit-seeking institutions is also undesirable. Undoubtedly, there have been (and probably still are) private schools which are reprehensible — either because they are failing to provide students with all that is promised by school representatives and printed catalogs, or because they only promise (and actually provide) rather insignificant training. Of course, these criticisms cannot be confined to profit-seeking schools; there are some tax-financed schools which are also "failures."

Only by recognizing the existence of the schools and their students and attempting to evaluate their performance can it be validly determined what training roles such schools can assume, and if they are indeed an untapped resource for training both disadvantaged and other persons.[7]

Estimated Numbers of Schools and Students

This study, which is concerned only with schools offering vocational training, disclosed an estimated total of about 7,000 schools with approximately 1.5 million students.[8]

[6] *Ibid.*, p. 131.

[7] Some elements of the evaluation of proprietary schools are presented in Chapter 4; Chapter 10 suggests the roles the schools could have in the field of vocational education.

[8] According to an estimate made in 1964, the number of private "specialty" schools exceeds 35,000 and is thus greater than the total number of public and private secondary schools, colleges and universities. Student enrollment was set at more than 5 million by Drs. Clark and Sloan. However, most of the schools in that study offered courses (or lessons) in "leisure-time activities" as well as employment-oriented courses. See Harold F. Clark and Harold S. Sloan, *Classrooms on Main Street* (New York: Teachers College Press, 1966), pp. 4, 126–38.

When the schools are divided into four generic occupational categories, the number of schools and student enrollments are as follows:[9]

TABLE 2–1

**ESTIMATED NUMBER OF PRIVATE VOCATIONAL SCHOOLS
AND STUDENTS IN THE U.S., 1966**

Occupational Category	Number of Schools	Percent of Schools	Number of Students	Percent of Students
Trade and Technical:				
—National Association of Trade and Technical Schools (NATTS)	151	2.1%	72,178	4.6%
—Non-NATTS Schools	2,849	40.3	763,532	48.8
	3,000	42.4	835,710	53.4
Business:				
—United Business Schools Association (UBSA)	500	7.1	199,500	12.8
—Non-UBSA Schools	800	11.3	240,000	15.3
	1,300	18.4	439,500	28.1
Cosmetology[a]	2,477	35.0	272,470	17.4
Barber[b]	294	4.2	15,876	1.0
	7,071	100.0%	1,563,556	99.9%

[a] Source for number of schools: *Milady State Board Cosmetology Guide,* Fifteenth Edition (Bronx, New York: Milady Publishing Corp., 1967).

[b] Source for number of schools: National Association of Barber Schools, Inc., "Barber Schools, Barber Students and Barber Statistics," Research Report No. 6A, 1968.

The trade and technical schools and their students are clearly the most sizable groups, accounting for 42 percent of all schools and 53 percent of all students. As shown later, these schools provide the greatest variety of training fields in the four broad categories. In addition, Chapter 3 reveals that about 45 percent of these schools require less than high school graduation for admission. All of these factors have led to selecting the trade and technical schools for special emphasis in this study. However, the schools of business, cosmetology and barbering also merit careful attention, since the employment prospects in all three occupational areas are generally promising; and many of these schools are prepared to train "disadvantaged" persons.

The preceding figures and those in the tables below provide at least some indication of the typical sizes of the different types of schools. For instance, only the cosmetology and barber schools have

[9] Rounding to 100 percent is not forced in the tables presented in this book.

total student enrollments which are proportionately lower than the total number of schools in these two categories. This was particularly true of the cosmetology schools which have an unusually large number of schools and a small average enrollment. Tables 2–2 through 2–6 are based primarily upon the responses of 1,194 schools, or 17 percent of the estimated total number of schools.[10]

Table 2–2 shows that nearly ⅔ of all responding trade and technical schools have 240 students or less. Only 6 percent of the schools have 721 students or more. The comparatively small average-size school (268 students) is considered representative of 2,849 trade and technical schools. The schools' small size, along with the great variety of courses, is an important explanation for the large number of these schools.

TABLE 2–2

STUDENT ENROLLMENTS: 416 TRADE AND TECHNICAL SCHOOLS IN 40 STATES

Number of Students	Number of Schools	Percent of Students
10–80	108	26.0%
81–160	120	28.8
161–240	40	9.6
241–320	33	7.9
321–400	35	8.4
401–560	32	7.6
561–720	22	5.3
721–1200	19	4.5
1201–2380	7	1.7
	416	99.8%

The 151 schools in the National Association of Trade and Technical Schools (NATTS) raise the count of trade and technical schools to 3,000. The average enrollment in these schools is 478, which is over 200 students more than the typical non-NATTS school. The distribution of students in Table 2–3 shows the differences in an even more striking way. Twenty-one schools in the last two intervals (721 students and over) account for nearly the same proportion of students in the NATTS schools that the first two intervals (10 to 160 students) do for the non-NATTS schools in Table 2–2.

At the same time, although the smaller NATTS schools (those with 10 to 240 students) account for only 12 percent of the students in Table 2–3, these schools represented more than ⅓ of the NATTS

---

[10] The results are derived from two different surveys and questionnaires. The "populations" are defined and the survey designs are discussed in Appendixes I and II; the appendixes also contain copies of the questionnaires.

TABLE 2–3

**STUDENT ENROLLMENTS: 127 NATTS TRADE AND
TECHNICAL SCHOOLS IN 31 STATES**

Number of Students	Number of Schools	Percent of Students
10–80	9	1.0%
81–160	15	3.2
161–240	22	7.5
241–320	21	9.7
321–400	18	11.1
401–560	16	12.5
561–720	5	5.3
721–1200	12	18.9
1201 and over	9	30.9
	127	100.1%

membership at the time of the survey. Although NATTS is a rather
new organization (established early in 1965), it would seem that
both large and small trade and technical schools are interested in
attaining the greater recognition that membership in an association
affords.

The average school associated with the United Business Schools
Association (UBSA) has an estimated enrollment of 399 students.
This figure is somewhat less than the typical NATTS school but it
represents some 500 members in an older association. The 800 schools
that are not members of UBSA were estimated to have an average
enrollment of 300 students. Therefore, as in the case of NATTS,
schools which are members of the business schools association tend
to be larger than the non-member schools.

Table 2–4 indicates the distribution of 381 schools (⅘ of which

TABLE 2–4

STUDENT ENROLLMENTS: 381 BUSINESS SCHOOLS IN 49 STATES

Number of Students	Number of Schools	Percent of Students
25–100	66	17.3%
101–200	93	24.4
201–300	63	16.5
301–400	46	12.1
401–500	28	7.3
501–600	25	6.6
601–700	13	3.4
701–900	12	3.1
901–1100	11	2.9
1101–1350	12	3.1
1351–4075	12	3.1
	381	99.8%

are members of UBSA) and their students on the basis of enrollment intervals. The relative importance of the small or average-size school is apparent here as it was for the non-member trade and technical schools in Table 2–2. Approximately 70 percent of the business students represented above were in schools having enrollments of 400 or less.

TABLE 2–5

STUDENT ENROLLMENTS: 181 COSMETOLOGY SCHOOLS IN 37 STATES

Number of Students	Number of Schools	Percent of Students
20–39	17	9.4%
40–79	57	31.5
80–119	44	24.2
120–159	34	18.8
160–199	8	4.4
200–259	11	6.1
260–419	7	3.9
420–750	3	1.7
	181	100.0%

The private cosmetology schools, which numbered 2,477 (or nearly twice the number of business schools) had an average annual enroll-ment of 110 students. A very large proportion (nearly 85%) of such schools was concentrated in the intervals enrolling 159 or less students annually (see Table 2–5). Nevertheless, these schools provide the bulk of training in this occupation; the public schools account for less than 15 percent of the total number of schools.

TABLE 2–6

STUDENT ENROLLMENTS: 89 BARBER SCHOOLS IN 28 STATES

Number of Students	Number of Schools	Percent of Students
12–19	8	9.0%
20–39	23	25.8
40–59	23	25.8
60–79	22	24.7
80–99	5	5.6
100–119	5	5.6
120–262	3	3.4
	89	99.9%

Barber schools, the smallest category with less than 300 schools, had the smallest average annual enrollment of 54 students per school. Approximately ¾ of the schools (and an even higher percentage of students) enrolled only 79 or less students in 1966 (see Table 2–6). Nearly 80 percent of all barber schools are *privately* operated and they account for an even higher percentage of the total barber school enrollment.[11]

The figures below summarize an important characteristic of school size for the four occupational categories:

66% of the trade and technical schools had enrollments of 240 or less.

70% of the business schools had enrollments of 400 or less.

85% of the cosmetology schools had enrollments of 159 or less.

75% of the barber schools had enrollments of 79 or less.

The large number of relatively small private vocational schools implies that their form of education is provided under generally competitive conditions. However, recent expansion in the franchising of schools and the corporate ownership of schools (discussed in Chapter 3) do demonstrate a greater concentration of administrative control.

Types of Courses Offered
in Trade and Technical Schools

The variety of occupational courses found in private trade and technical schools reflects their unique ability to respond to the training needs of many industries and professions.[12] About 230 different occupational courses were offered in the 544 trade and technical schools (128 NATTS schools and 416 non-members) examined earlier in this chapter. Since most schools offered more than one course, the total number of courses offered in these schools was nearly 1,500.[13]

The six major categories (based on the number of courses in each category) are:

	No. of Courses
Automobile Maintenance and related Services	127
Data Processing	185
Drafting	131
Electronics	159
Medical Services	154
Radio-TV	95
	851

[11] The remaining schools are about equally divided between public schools and penal institutions. See National Association of Barber Schools, Inc., *op. cit.*

[12] In addition to the courses considered here, more than 15 different types of courses in the secretarial, office machine and office management occupations were listed by trade and technical schools. Since such courses are offered principally in business schools, they have been excluded here.

[13] If the average number of courses reported by the NATTS schools had prevailed for the non-member schools, the total would have been closer to 2,000

Less than 60 percent of all courses are included in the above categories, although the three largest areas of training (data processing, electronics and medical services) are acknowledged to be growth fields in most manpower projections. The other three categories cannot necessarily be designated "traditional," because drafting may be allied with the electronics industry and a radio-TV course may emphasize the repair of color television sets. Even automobile repair offers numerous employment openings for competent workers.[14]

Additional important fields include courses in: commercial arts; construction; fashion design, needle trades and shoemaking; food processing, merchandising, preparation and service; interior design and related services; major and minor appliance repair and servicing; machine shop; photography; printing; sales, promotions and related services; tool and die design; various forms of transportation and traffic management; and welding. Finally, courses in aerospace engineering technology, waste and water reconversion, gardening, hotel-motel management and related services, and many others, though listed only by a few schools, are areas of growing job opportunities.

Not all of the courses (which are listed in the appendix to this chapter) are equivalent to generally accepted occupational designations.[15] At the same time, occupational breakdowns are necessarily somewhat arbitrary. For example, is automobile body and fender repair only a part of automobile maintenance, which also includes mechanics, air conditioning, front end and wheel alignment, automotive damage appraisal, and several other skill categories? The answer is "yes." At the least, therefore, should not a body and fender repair course include (as a minimum) a course in automotive damage appraisal so that a repairman can progress to that position and eventually even to the ownership of a shop? The answer is "yes," "no," or "maybe."[16] This depends upon a person's interest, ability, or willingness to devote the additional time to a course in damage appraisal.

It is clear that numerous alternatives can arise with respect to almost any course. A course that is designated as only *part* of an

---

courses. Many of the respondents to the short questionnaire listed only general training categories — such as communications or automotives.

[14] Customer complaints about repairs have been investigated by the Senate Antitrust and Monopoly Subcommittee. See *The New York Times*, December 6, 1968, p. 1.

[15] Also, technical experts were generally not consulted in compiling the list of courses; therefore some courses which were the same may have been given a separate listing.

[16] Vale Technical Institute in Blairsville, Pennsylvania has an automobile wrecking service associated with the school, which offers courses for auto mechanic, body and fender repairman, automotive damage appraisal, and several other specialties.

occupation could involve upgrading for a person who was previously considered incapable of being more than a lumper. Another person may enroll in a short course because he knows that the earnings are quite high; and he only wants to be employed in the position long enough to accumulate the savings he needs to enter a completely different business or perhaps to attend college. Another student may be pursuing a plan that includes the expectation of on-the-job training and enrollment in additional occupational courses following the completion of a rather specific course. Unfortunately there are also some persons enrolled in courses unsuitable for them because they were unwisely counseled (or not counseled at all) in either the public or private school they attended.

APPENDIX TO CHAPTER 2

TYPES OF COURSES OFFERED IN 544 REPORTING TRADE AND TECHNICAL SCHOOLS

	No. of Courses	
AUTO MAINTENANCE AND RELATED SERVICES		
Appraiser — Auto Damage	2	
Attendant — Service Station	3	
Mechanic —		
Basic and Master	50	
Diesel	6	
Salesman — Parts Counter	1	
Specialist —		
Air Conditioning	8	
Automatic Transmission	13	
Body and Fender Repair	22	
Conventional and Power Brakes	4	
Front End and Wheel Alignment	6	
Engine Tune-Up	12	127
COMMERCIAL ARTS		
Artist — Commercial	31	
Consultant — Color	1	
Designer —		
Greeting Card	2	
Textile	3	
Glass Blower — Neon	1	
Illustrator —		
Children's	1	
Fashion	8	
General	11	
Letterer	1	
Painter — Sign	2	61
CONSTRUCTION		
Building Craftsman —		
Electrician	8	
Heavy Equipment Operator and Mechanic	5	
Mason	2	
Painter	1	
Plumber and Pipefitter	3	

	No. of Courses	
CONSTRUCTION (*cont.*)		
Building Craftsmen (*cont.*)		
Steamfitter	1	
Structural Iron Worker	1	
Cabinetmaker (incls. Woodworking Techniques)	7	
"Engineer" —		
Architectural Aide	3	
Civil Aide	1	
Construction Technician	3	
Estimator	3	
Maintenance Man —		
Technician	2	
Superintendent	1	41
DATA PROCESSING		
Computer Maintenance	23	
Computer Programmer	76	
Data Processer (incls. Keypunch and Tab Operator)	86	185
DRAFTING		
Blueprint Reader	6	
Draftsman —		
General (incls. basic, intermediate and advanced)	44	
Architectural	16	
Electro-Mechanical	4	
Electronic and Electrical	16	
Engineering	13	
Mechanical	22	
Structural	6	
Illustrator — Technical	3	
Renderer — Architectural	1	131
DRYCLEANING AND LAUNDRY		
Drycleaner	3	
Helper — Laundry	2	
Manager — Drycleaning	2	
Presser — Laundry/Factory	2	
Spotter	1	10
ELECTRONICS[a]		
Servicer	22	

[a] Some of the courses offered in this field include training in data processing. At the other extreme, some might have been more appropriately placed under the less dramatic headings of "Electrical" or "Electricity," but this was impossible to determine from the titles as reported.

	No. of Courses	
ELECTRONICS (*cont.*)		
Technician[b]	137	159
FASHION DESIGN, NEEDLE TRADES AND SHOEMAKING		
Buyer — Assistant	3	
Designer — Fashion and Assistant Fashion	12	
Dressmaker	9	
Fitter	2	
Patternmaker and Grader	10	
Repairman/Rebuilder — Power Sewing Machine	1	
Sewer —		
Needle Trades	9	
Power Machine	4	
Shoemaker/Shoe Repairman	2	
Tailor and Alterer	11	63
FLORISTRY AND GROUNDSKEEPING		
Designer — Floral	3	
Groundsworker —		
Gardener	2	
Landscaper	1	
Nursery Worker	1	
Retailer —		
Florist	3	
Sales Clerk	2	
Shopowner	2	14
FOOD PREPARATION, PROCESSING, SERVICE AND MERCHANDISING		
Preparation —		
Baker	1	
Chef	3	
Kitchen Helper	2	
Processing —		
Meat Cutter	6	
Meat Wrapper	2	
Retailing —		
Cashier, Grocery Stocker and Checker	6	
Market Manager	2	

[b] Electronics Technician courses prepare for work in a broad variety of occupational settings — including manufacturing plants, laboratories, consulting firms, construction, etc.

	No. of Courses	
FOOD PREPARATION PROCESSING, SERVICE **AND MERCHANDISING** (*cont.*)		
Service —		
Dietetics and Food Service Management	2	
Waiter	1	25
FUNERAL WORK		
Embalmer	3	
Funeral Director	3	6
HOTEL/MOTEL OPERATION		
Maintenance Personnel —		
Executive and House Steward	1	
Housekeeping	2	
Manager	5	
Office Personnel —		
Accountant and Cashier	2	
Clerk	1	
PBX Operator	1	12
INDUSTRIAL MANAGEMENT		
"Engineer" — Time Study	2	
Manager — Industrial (Industrial Mgmt. Techniques)	5	7
INTERIOR DESIGN AND RELATED SERVICES		
Designer —		
Interior	10	
Furniture	1	
Related-Skill Workers —		
Carpet Layer	1	
Drapery Maker	2	
Linoleum — Tile Floor Layer	1	
Slipcover Maker	2	
Upholsterer	4	21
INVESTIGATION		
Fire and Explosion	1	
General	1	
Insurance	1	3
JEWELRY DESIGN AND REPAIR		
Diamond Setter	4	
Jewelry Maker and Repairman	2	
Watch Worker (incls. elementary and advanced; also includes engraving)	7	13

	No. of Courses	
MACHINE SHOP		
(Includes courses in layout, operation and inspection, as well as basic machines)	30	30
MAJOR AND MINOR APPLIANCE REPAIR AND SERVICING		
Technician — Air Conditioning-Refrigeration-Heating	9	
Repairman —		
Electric Motor	6	
Master Appliance	4	
Office Machine	2	
Small Appliance	3	
Serviceman —		
Air Conditioning	12	
Oil Burner	5	
Refrigeration	12	53
MEDICAL SERVICES		
Aide —		
Geriatric	1	
Home Health	1	
Hospital	2	
Institutional	1	
Nursing	4	
Pediatric	1	
Assistant —		
Dental	25	
Doctor's Office	3	
Laboratory	3	
Medical	24	
Examiner — Medical Claims	1	
Hygienist — Dental	1	
Nurse —		
Licensed Vocational	1	
Practical	8	
Orderly	1	
Secretary — Medical[c]	23	
Technician —		
Dental	8	
Laboratory	9	
Medical	13	
Optical	1	

[c] Although, as previously explained, any other listing of office occupations is excluded, an exception is made for *medical secretary* because it is assumed that a principal part of this training leads to technical proficiency.

No. of
Courses

MEDICAL SERVICES (*cont.*)

Technologist —
Dental	17	
X-Ray	6	154

PERFORMING ARTS

Performer — Dance, Music (incls. opera and concert singing), Theater (incls. cinema, stage and TV acting)	6	
Dramatist — Radio/TV	1	
Speaker	1	8

PERSONAL SERVICES

Finishing — Personal	3	
Modeling	5	
Swedish Massage	1	9

PHOTOGRAPHY

Photographer —
Commercial	3	
Medical	1	
Motion Picture	1	
Newspaper	1	
Portrait	4	
Printer/Retoucher —
Airbrush Technique	1	
Colorist	3	
Dye-Transfer Printing	1	
Negative Retouching	2	
Repairman — Camera	1	18

PRINTING

Artist — Graphic	5	
Assistant — General Print Shop	1	
Letterpress —
Hand Composition	1	
Pressman	1	
Linotype Maintenance	3	
Linotype Operator	4	
Monotype Keyboard and Casting Machine Operator	1	
Lithography —
Lithographer	1	
Multilith Operator	1	
Offset Cameraman	1	
Offset Printing	2	
Photolithographer	1	

		No. of *Courses*
PRINTING (*cont.*)		
Lithography (*cont.*)		
Platemaker	1	
Pressman	2	
Stripper	1	
Silkscreen Technician	1	27
RECREATION AND SPORTS		
Athletic Trainer	1	
Bartender	1	
Baseball Personnel —		
Business Manager	1	
Scorekeeper (also incls. softball scorekeeping)	1	
Umpire	2	
Farrier (incls. some veterinary courses)	1	
Gunsmith	1	8
RADIO-TV		
Broadcaster	19	
Repairman	34	
Salesman	2	
Technician —		
Communications (incls. preparation for FCC license)	39	
Color TV	1	95
SALES, PROMOTIONS AND RELATED SERVICES		
Promotion —		
Advertiser	5	
Copywriter	2	
Market Research	1	
Public Relations	1	
Sales —		
Auctioneer	2	
Merchandising	2	
Professional Salesmanship	1	
Sales and Management	7	21
TOOL AND DIE DESIGN		
(Includes plastic molding courses; also includes both separate and combined courses — i.e., certain schools offer separate courses in tool design and die design, others combine them with one another and/or with tool and die making.)	54	54

	No. of Courses	
TRANSPORTATION — AIR		
Administrator — Aviation Specialist	2	
Communications — FAA	6	
Flight and Operations Personnel —		
Auxiliary —		
Dispatcher	1	
Hostess	6	
Instruments	1	
Ramp Agent	1	
Technician — Airframe Power Plant Mechanic	7	
Technician — Radar	1	
Pilot	5	
Office Personnel —		
Airline Travel Agency	4	
International Travel	1	
Reservationist	12	47
TRANSPORTATION — FREIGHT		
Supervisor —		
Cargo	4	
Freight Claim	1	
Rate Analyst	1	6
TRANSPORTATION — HIGHWAY		
Driver —		
Bus	1	
Truck —		
Diesel	2	
Heavy	1	
Straight	1	
Tractor Trailer	2	7
TRANSPORTATION — SEA		
Ship Builder	1	
Shipboard Personnel —		
Deck Officer — Merchant Marine	2	
"Engineer" — Marine	1	
Pilot — Merchant Marine	2	
Technician — Navigational	2	
Underwater Operations Personnel —		
Decompression Chamber Operator	2	
Deep Sea Diver	1	11

	No. of Courses	
TRANSPORTATION — SPACE		
Technician — Aerospace Engineering	2	2
TRANSPORTATION — TRAFFIC MANAGEMENT		
Traffic Manager	5	
Transportation Specialist	4	9
WASTE RECONVERSION		
Technician — Waste and Wastewater	1	1
WELDING		
Welder —		
General	23	
Arc	9	
Arc and Acetylene Combination	3	
Electric	1	
Gas	2	
Heli-Arc	6	
Oxy-Acetylene	6	
Pipe	4	54
TOTAL COURSES		1,483

CHAPTER 3

Flexible Operation and Organization

"We made many expensive mistakes the first year (1964) or so by being too idealistic and having no one to refer to due to the uniqueness of our school; but now we've developed a pattern of operations that runs very smoothly."

— PEG HOOVER, Secretary-Treasurer,
Porterville Horseshoeing School, Inc.
Porterville, California

Flexible accommodation to the needs and demands of students and their prospective employers is the outstanding operative feature of private vocational schools. Indeed, like any private business firm, the survival and growth of the schools have been possible only because the schools have successfully satisfied their "consumers."

The objective of school owners and administrators is to prepare their students for employment. This objective is as defined as the school's goal of making profits, which are, of course, necessary to stay "in business." The profit motive is tempered by the need to provide suitable training; hence, the quest for profits serves to stimulate continuous changes in operation and instruction. Mr. Milton Willenson, former President of the Private Vocational Schools Association of New York, is convinced that private vocational schools cannot survive unless they continue to revamp their programs. In fact, some of the older schools have managed to survive only by successfully introducing *new* occupational courses.

This chapter is concerned mainly with several of the changes or innovations which proprietary schools have instituted, innovations which by now have become standard procedure in most schools. Some of the practices, e.g., operating schools on a year-round basis, are unique to these schools. Others are being considered and even embraced as worthwhile "innovations" by public schools. A previous record for adapting to student and employer needs justifies the expectation of future innovations in the private schools.

Rationales for the Existence
of Private Vocational Schools

Thoughtful persons who are also knowledgeable about the policies and procedures of private vocational schools believe that the schools have succeeded because they fill gaps which are not met by other training resources. According to Dr. John S. McCauley of the U. S. Department of Labor, proprietary schools are virtually uninvolved in training persons for occupations in agriculture because the public vocational schools effectively meet requirements of students and the industry. On the other hand, public secondary schools only recently became involved in the field of office occupations; private business schools providing such training have therefore flourished.

In addition to providing programs within certain broad occupational fields that are absent from public instruction, the private schools institute courses that seem to be unfeasible for the public school systems. Many private school classes, for example, have small student enrollments at any given time; also, course materials can often be completed in a comparatively short time. The same courses could evidently not be as easily or quickly assimilated in the public schools, given their larger enrollments and longer courses. Private schools are also able to organize programs related to industries and even single firms that have achieved sudden prominence. Data processing is such a field. It is a field, moreover, that demands very costly equipment; and some of the larger manufacturers of the equipment have expeditiously established their own schools. Private schools also offer courses in occupations whose employment opportunities extend beyond a school's geographic location; the public schools are less likely to offer such courses.

Even when vocational education is available in the high schools, it may be deficient in either quantitative or qualitative terms. For instance, students in the public schools may be unable to register in courses where the enrollments are at capacity, and they leave school prematurely because of lack of interest in or aptitude for academic programs.[1] Many of these students have been attracted to the very specific training offered in private schools. Other students, including high school graduates, enroll in the proprietary schools because their previous vocational education was "generally little more than preliminary";[2] and public post-secondary or two-year community

[1] Apart from the problem of capacity enrollment, high school students can also not be accommodated should they alter their plans for vocational education after a deadline date for applications established by the school.

[2] Harold F. Clark and Harold S. Sloan, *Classrooms on Main Street* (New York: Columbia University Teachers College Press, 1966), pp. 4–5.

colleges are still not readily available in most states. (Even if they were, some persons would still prefer the shorter courses found in the private schools.)

It is apparent therefore that private and public schools have often been "non-competitive groups"; at other times they may be more nearly in direct competition. The private schools have been leaders in training handicapped persons, and this has often involved the design of highly individualized courses and techniques. Although the programs in the two types of institutions are presumably similar, differences still exist. For example, the private school instructors invariably teach only those mathematical principles which are directly related to and necessary for mastery of a specific occupation; the public school curriculum is more likely to include a broader treatment of the subject.

A study of the structure and functioning of the two types of school systems is actually the principal way of differentiating the schools. Private schools are market-oriented; school officials are in constant contact with employers and industrial associations. The owner or training director of a private school is free to quickly implement the revision of a course or the introduction of a new course; and new programs are usually directly financed out of retained earnings or highly liquid assets. "Indicators" for change are usually perceived more slowly in the public schools, which must moreover secure approval of school boards and local or state educators and legislators.

Flexible Operations: Student Needs

The flexibility and adaptability of private schools naturally applies to accommodations made for students whose tuition is virtually the entire source of school income. The schools have not only devised training courses which are unavailable elsewhere, but many of the schools also recognize that it can be profitable for both school and student to offer courses that do not require a high school education. Day and evening sessions and practically year-round operating schedules are a second important means of adjusting to student needs. These procedures enable numerous aspiring students with educational and financial limitations to attend school for either short and intensive or, contrariwise, for rather long periods of time.

Admission Requirements

Although this book deals mainly with *trade* and *technical* schools and their students, it is important to include at least some of the findings on the schools of *barbering, business* and *cosmetology.* For when all types of schools are considered, the range and diversity in student admission requirements become apparent.

It is most striking (in an era of steadily growing emphasis upon formal education) that 514 out of 1,186 reporting private vocational schools throughout the nation (43 percent) indicated either directly or by implication that one or more of their courses require less than a high school education for admission. Moreover, 23 percent of all schools had course(s) requiring only nine years or less of schooling.[3]

As a group, the barber schools have somewhat lower educational requirements than the three other groups. Indeed, about 82 percent of the barber schools that responded to a postcard questionnaire[4] indicated that their courses require less than a high school education for admission. Another 10 percent of the schools require of their students only the "ability to read and write." This means that only 8 percent of the responding schools demand a high school diploma (or its equivalent) for admission.

TABLE 3–1

MINIMUM EDUCATIONAL REQUIREMENTS FOR ADMISSION
TO 89 SCHOOLS OF BARBERING IN 28 STATES

Minimum Years of Education Required	Number of Schools	Percent of Schools
None	2	2.2%
1–6	1	1.1
7–9	38	42.7
10–11	32	36.0
12 (High school graduation or its equivalent)	7	7.9
Other[a]	9	10.1
Totals	89	100.0%

[a] Seven schools require "ability to read and write."

The typical cosmetology school answering the questionnaire indicated only slightly higher educational standards for admission than the barber schools. About 91 percent of these schools (listed below) state directly or by implication that one or more of their courses requires less than a high school education for admission. As in the case of the barber schools, more than 40 percent of the schools required no more than nine years of schooling.

[3] These total results include 128 members of the National Association of Trade and Technical Schools (NATTS); the NATTS schools are considered separately following the discussion of trade and technical schools in Table 3–4.
[4] See Exhibit 1 in Appendix I.

TABLE 3–2

MINIMUM EDUCATIONAL REQUIREMENTS FOR ADMISSION TO
180 SCHOOLS OF COSMETOLOGY IN 37 STATES

Minimum Years of Education Required	Number of Schools	Percent of Schools
None	3	1.7%
1–6	—	—
7–9	71	39.4
10–11	77	42.8
12 (High School graduation or its equivalent)	17	9.4
Other[a]	12	6.7
Totals	180	100.1%

[a] Most of these responses refer to age requirements.

The level of education required for admission to business schools is almost completely the reverse of that demanded of entering barber and cosmetology students. Table 3–3 shows that nearly 90 percent of the responding business schools in 49 states require high school

TABLE 3–3

MINIMUM EDUCATIONAL REQUIREMENTS FOR ADMISSION
TO 378 BUSINESS SCHOOLS IN 49 STATES

Minimum Years of Education Required	Number of Schools	Percent of Schools
None	2	.5%
1–6	—	—
7–9	11	2.9
10–11	20	5.3
12 (High School graduation or its equivalent)[a]	335	88.6
Other	10	2.6
Totals	378	99.9%

[a] 50 of these schools indicated their acceptance of a high school diploma or its equivalent for admission.

graduation or its equivalent for admission. A small number of the schools stated they have lowered entrance requirements for students financed under the Vocational Rehabilitation Act[5] or for applicants who are able to pass a school-administered aptitude test. The United

[5] The Washington agency administering the Act, formerly known as the Vocational Rehabilitation Administration, has been redesignated the Rehabilitation Services Administration (RSA). Agencies and programs at the state and local levels retain the name Vocational Rehabilitation.

Business Schools Association (UBSA) has received a "demonstration" contract for several of its member schools in 17 states under the Manpower Development and Training Act (MDTA). Although the schools affiliated with UBSA do require high school graduation for admission, there presumably have been some non-graduates in at least that phase of the MDTA project which makes provision for remedial courses in basic education and cooperative work-study arrangements. Adjustments to actual student qualifications coincide with the views of the administrator of a large business school which also franchises a secretarial course to about 500 schools. He believes that many schools have unstated, informal ways of selection and they "may very well admit a fair number of persons who are not high school graduates." Finally, the study by Clark and Sloan disclosed a similar conclusion with respect to one-year business schools:

> Although a high-school diploma, or its equivalent, is usually prescribed as an entrance requirement, this regulation is interpreted liberally. Ability to profit from the instruction rates high among the possible equivalencies, especially for older students with some business experience. There may be a sprinkling of terminal elementary-school graduates, but most of the students have had some high-school training.[6]

Entrance requirements to trade and technical schools, which offer a wide variety of occupational courses, fall somewhere between the extremes of the three preceding types of schools considered. Table 3–4 shows that the schools requiring no high school diploma (or its equivalent) total 36 percent; 12 percent of all schools actually have no minimum education requirements. The category of "other" requirements generally implies much less than a high school diploma and includes age or physical requirements or assessment of the applicants' capabilities by school officials — "ability to handle tools"; "sewing aptitude"; "ability to benefit from training"; "ability to speak, read and write." Altogether then, about 44 percent of the trade and technical schools (in 40 states) have at least one course that requires less than a high school education for admission; in contrast, the business schools shown in Table 3–3 claimed only one-fourth of this percentage.

Eighteen percent of the trade and technical schools that require a high school education specified that an applicant would also be accepted with a high school equivalency. About 15 percent of the business schools also offer this explicit option. Undoubtedly, a considerably higher percentage of both types of schools waive the formal high school requirement.

[6] Clark and Sloan, *Classrooms*, pp. 37–38.

TABLE 3–4

**MINIMUM EDUCATIONAL REQUIREMENTS FOR ADMISSION
TO 411 TRADE AND TECHNICAL SCHOOLS IN 40 STATES**

Minimum Years of Education Required	*Number of Responding*	*Percent of Schools*
None	49	11.9%
1–6	9	2.2
7–9	53	12.9
10–11	37	9.0
12 (High School graduation or its equivalent)[a]	232	56.4
Other	31	7.5
Totals	411	99.9%

[a] 42 of these schools indicated their acceptance of either a high school diploma or its equivalent for admission.

The preceding findings on trade and technical schools do not include the responses of 128 members of the National Association of Trade and Technical Schools (NATTS) located in 31 states. Since most of the schools have confidently joined the Association mainly for the purpose of ultimately receiving accreditation (and approval, in general), it is interesting to compare their admission requirements with those of the nonmember schools in Table 3–4.

Fourteen percent of the nonmember trade and technical schools have courses that require six years of education or less; nine percent of the NATTS schools are in this category. However, NATTS schools requiring less than high school graduation for admission total 45 percent (see Table 3–5);[7] this ratio compares with 44 percent for the nonmember schools shown in Table 3–4.

The Association schools were further requested to indicate their minimum educational requirement for admission to each course, and the results also appear in Table 3–5. The percentages, by courses, for each of the first four categories are less than the percentages on the basis of school. Altogether, 37 percent of the courses require less than high school graduation for admission, whereas 45 percent of the schools have at least one course falling in the same classification.

Although flexibility in admission requirements can naturally be beneficial to applicants with limited formal education, the variability in admission standards may not always be considered in the best interests of a school. For example, the administrators of a school

[7] The minimum educational requirement listed by each school does not necessarily apply to all courses offered by the school.

TABLE 3–5

MINIMUM EDUCATIONAL REQUIREMENTS FOR ADMISSION TO
128 NATTS TRADE AND TECHNICAL SCHOOLS IN 31 STATES,
BY SCHOOL AND INDIVIDUAL COURSE

Minimum Years of Education Required	*By Responding Schools*		*By Courses*	
	Number	*Percent*	*Number*	*Percent*
None	11	8.6%	30	6.2%
1–6	1	.8	2	.4
7–9	27	21.1	82	17.0
10–11	18	14.1	64	13.3
12 (High School graduation or its equivalent)	70	54.7	294	61.0
12+	1	.8	10	2.1
Totals	128	100.1%	482	100.0%

for computer programming, which has issued more than 90 franchises, will not consider an applicant who lacks at least high school equivalency. The school's officers feel that a person who will not persevere for such an achievement ("which is not that hard") is unlikely to be adequately motivated to complete a programming course.

Nevertheless, the availability of various types of private vocational schools with low educational requirements for admission should be of considerable relevance to the administrators of government programs designed to train disadvantaged persons. Undoubtedly, persons lacking the effective demand (i.e., ability to pay) for such training programs comprise an even larger group than those who have thus far benefited from the training.

Additional Admission Requirements

Applicants for admission to some of the NATTS schools may also be required to: 1) pass an achievement or aptitude test; 2) fulfill certain age, physical or other requirements.

Achievement or aptitude tests are defended as a necessity by some school administrators, because the capabilities of their applicants vary widely despite similar schooling; and such differences may not be readily discernible. One school administrator states his problem succinctly: "I must assume that a high school graduate can add, subtract and divide; but this is an erroneous assumption." High school "graduates" may moreover be unable to read, write or follow instructions. Therefore this school — and undoubtedly others — will not accept all high school graduates; on the other hand, a person with only an eighth grade education, who has worked in a television repair shop and has also read widely, may qualify for admission.

Some of the better schools that take a "long-run" view of their achievements also believe it can be in the best interests of both students and future employers to administer aptitude tests. It is reasoned that many employers — in the electronic computer programming field, for example — are extremely reluctant to hire persons who lack a college education, since they expect their employees to qualify for consistent promotions. A student may have only a high school education; but, it is argued, he may score highly on aptitude tests which are supposed to measure abilities to solve problems and conceptualize logically. If so, he is much more likely to pass a programming course with high grades and then secure employment plus occupational advances.

Furthermore, individuals who do not score high enough to be accepted for a particular course may still be able to gain admission to a school. This is naturally only true of schools with diversified courses or similar courses that prepare for different levels of proficiency within the same or related occupation.[8] Numerous trade and technical schools and other types of vocational schools do in fact offer such opportunities.[9] For example, schools that prepare "high-level" engineering technicians may also offer instruction for industrial or service technicians.[10]

About 47 percent of all the occupational courses offered by the responding NATTS schools call for a passing grade in an achievement or aptitude test. Many of these tests measure practical skills. For example, a school that instructs in automobile mechanics provides applicants with a set of tools and step-by-step instructions on how to perform actual operations on an automobile carburetor, generator or starter. A California school with courses for medical or dental assistants and practical nurses requires basic typing. Manual dexterity or mechanical comprehension tests must be passed at some of the schools that train dental technicians and automobile mechanics. Other students must secure a satisfactory score on a general intelli-

[8] Testing at the Opportunities Industrialization Centers of Philadelphia and other cities is distinct because a training program is available for virtually every applicant. This is considered a "screening-in" process and it is discussed in the section dealing with counseling.

[9] One typical school trains in three occupational areas: drafting, television service and repair, and auto mechanics. The requirement for drafting (architectural, mechanical or structural) is either two years of high school or two or more years of practical experience in allied trades. Graduation from junior high school or satisfactory educational equivalent is required for the television service and repair course. There is no definite requirement for automobile mechanics other than a written test to determine elementary reading comprehension and mechanical ability.

[10] See Ken Gilmore, "Operation Activate," *Electronics Experimenter's Handbook*, Fall Edition 1966, p. 79.

gence test in order to study electronics technology. An IQ test is administered at a school that trains draftsmen and various technicians, as well as a few secretarial classifications.

The oft-mentioned diversity of the private schools is evident at the United Electronics Institute, which has schools in Louisville, Kentucky, Des Moines, Iowa, and Akron, Ohio. A student enrolling in these schools must complete pre-entrance training at home consisting of eight "technical assignments plus other related materials" before beginning the residential phase of training.

Age, Physical and Other Requirements

In addition to minimum educational requirements, the private schools may set other requirements for age, physical condition and a miscellaneous grouping, which are less easy to quantify precisely.

Nearly 40 percent of all the courses offered by the NATTS schools have an age requirement for admission. When an age was stated, however, it was usually a minimum entrance age of 17 or 18, and the figure was probably related to state laws on public school attendance.[11] Some schools have admitted 16-year old youngsters with the approval of public education officials. Usually, according to the head of instruction at one school, these young persons are accepted only if they did not like school but do enjoy "tinkering." The number of such young people enrolled at the NATTS schools cannot be estimated. Even less is known about the extent to which young persons attending public schools are also enrolled in private schools in the afternoons or evenings; the number is probably relatively small.

Only one school listed an upper age limit, and this was in response to the maximum age (45 years) at which one may qualify for licensing as a welder. Other schools undoubtedly have maximum age limits. However, the limits are generally comparatively high, since the average maximum age of students enrolled in the 128 schools was 48.

The physical and miscellaneous requirements listed by most schools generally concerned the potential employability of the applicants in private or public enterprise. Therefore several schools stated that no student would be accepted if he had a physical disability that would limit his chances of finding a training-related job after completion of a course.[12]

[11] Actually, it is compulsory in 41 states for students to attend school through age 16. See August W. Steinhilber and Carl J. Sokolowski, *State Law on Compulsory Attendance*, OE-23044 (Washington: U. S. Office of Education, 1966), p. 11.

[12] Schools answered as follows: "applicants must be employable"; "placement must be feasible"; "applicant must be able to pass average industrial physical examination."

Some of the physical requirements have been established by public regulatory agencies. The United States Coast Guard examination must be passed by persons enrolling in a course for ship radio officer; the physical examination of the Interstate Commerce Commission, plus a commercial driver's license, are requirements for tractor-trailer training; and commercial pilot training cannot be undertaken without receipt of a Federal Aviation Agency Medical Certificate. Besides commercial pilots, evidently only certified pipewelders must pass a physical examination every six months; and the welders are required to pass a proficiency examination frequently. These welders may work on steam pipes that need to withstand several hundred pounds of pressure — an exceptionally exacting task. Yet, of the two NATTS schools providing this training, one accepts persons with a third grade education and the other accepts retarded persons.[13]

Other specifications are based upon a school's knowledge of employer standards. Hence manual dexterity, muscular coordination or ability to handle tools are often listed as requirements for occupations in machine shops, air conditioning and refrigeration, automobile body repair and painting, and medical laboratories. Color blindness disqualifies for some positions in photography and electronics; but corrected vision is acceptable for training in welding and drafting. Students enrolled in various medical and dental occupations naturally must be in generally good health.

Several schools will not enroll persons with "emotional disturbances" or "mental handicaps." On the other hand, many schools stated that their physical requirements vary because they train students referred by their state Vocational Rehabilitation (VR) agency. A school of drafting that has done considerable training for a VR agency indicated explicitly that mental or nervous disorders are *not* disqualifications for training. The Nashville Auto Diesel College in Nashville, Tennessee has accepted handicapped persons from more than 20 states.

Although about 42 percent of the courses have physical requirements for entrance, the exact figure is probably somewhat higher, since several schools insist upon having personal interviews with prospective students. Such interviews are, however, only partly concerned with attempting to spot physical or emotional disabilities. One school tries to evaluate ". . . ability to follow instructions, interest in subject matter, and degree of motivation toward achievement of goals." Another school finds that a ". . . personal interview determines the applicant's qualifications for working closely with

[13] A certified pipewelder leaves his mark or signature on a job and welders often recognize each other's marks and sometimes even their welds.

others and communicating concepts and programs." At times, the requirement is merely to "be able to read, write and understand English."

In addition to the educational requirements mentioned earlier, some schools are concerned with a student's previous experience, or his interest in completing more than the preliminary portion of an occupational course. For instance, a course in machine design requires a minimum of two years' drafting experience. Another school seeks to establish whether a student who is admitted to a course in automobile mechanics will be likely to strive for a grade high enough to qualify him for a diesel engine course.

Even after acceptance to a school there may be a trial period for both the "borderline" student and the school. At least one school offers each student the option of leaving after the first week at no charge. A school for dental assistants and technicians and another for automobile mechanics have 30-day trial periods for each student.

School Attendance Schedules

The heterogeneity of admission requirements to private vocational schools is matched by great variation in school attendance schedules. These include class starting intervals, the number of weeks schools operate annually, and, frequently, alternatives of day or evening and full- or part-time attendance.

Qualified applicants are accepted in many vocational courses at highly frequent intervals. This is a very useful service for persons who must work full-time, for an indefinite period of time. Another group that is well-served by this procedure is disadvantaged persons who are referred to private vocational schools by Vocational Rehabilitation agencies. These physically or emotionally handicapped individuals often cannot adjust to a postponement which could involve several weeks or even months; the expeditious processing of an application and the commencement of training within a matter of a few days is indeed likely to be considered a victory by such an applicant.

Table 3–6 presents the intervals at which new classes are convened in 83 trade and technical schools. More than 50 percent of the reporting schools have courses that accept students at least as often as once every two months. Fourteen of the schools indicated that they actually enroll new students every week — i.e., every Monday (or Tuesday if a holiday falls on Monday); such frequent convening of new classes makes it particularly feasible to accommodate slow learners at those schools that allow a student to attend as long as it is required for him to become proficient.

TABLE 3–6

CLASS STARTING INTERVALS FOR 83 NATTS SCHOOLS[a]

Frequency of Class Starts	Number of Schools
weekly	14
monthly	7
every 5 weeks	9
every 6 weeks	5
6 times annually	8
4 times annually	17
3 times annually	14
twice annually	7
once annually	2
	83

[a] Information was secured from school catalogs.

Mr. William Goddard, Executive Director of NATTS, believes that the starting intervals are even more frequent than the average represented in Table 3–6. On the basis of a larger number of schools, he estimates that the majority of schools have four new classes annually, but they may accept students on a *monthly* basis.[14]

Several schools, without stating so directly, implied that students are accepted for certain courses at various intervals throughout the year. Their catalogs read as follows:

— ". . . students may enroll as soon as space or equipment becomes available."

— ". . . . classes begin periodically in response to enrollment demand."

— "There is no long waiting period to begin."

As discussed further in Chapter 6, new students can be accepted at frequent intervals only because the schools' instructors can presumably respond to the challenges that are entailed. Such challenges are minimized to the extent that a vocational course requires students, for the most part, to perform individually in a shop setting, rather than as note-takers in a classroom. Nevertheless, special accommodations are still required of a school and its staff. (During a visit to a welding school, a student sponsored under the Manpower Development and Training Act was heard thanking the school's president for allowing him to make up the training assignments he had missed due to a long illness.)

[14] The training programs in Sweden have some of the flexibility found in the private vocational schools in the United States; starting dates are frequent, according to Mr. Sol Swerdloff of the U. S. Department of Labor.

In addition to adjusting to student needs during the training period, the frequent starting intervals for many courses may have advantages for graduates seeking full-time jobs. A school owner observed that students at many private schools are "turned out almost every week"; they enter the labor market, therefore, in relatively moderate numbers and not as part of large graduating classes converging on employers once or twice yearly.

Weeks of Operation Annually

Once a serious student enrolls in a private school, he can attend classes virtually on a year-round basis. The following figures show that 124 out of the 128 reporting NATTS schools provide instruction at least 48 weeks during the year.

Number of Weeks Courses Are Available	Number of Schools
52	50
48–51	74
26–47	4
	128

Like class scheduling practices already discussed, this one can benefit students who feel compelled to complete their training in the shortest feasible time.

An experiment in the State of New York has demonstrated that the students attending school 40 additional days annually ". . . made proportionately greater academic gains than those on the conventional schedule, especially in reading. And the low-ability pupils made proportionately greater progress than the average and bright." It was therefore concluded that "greater continuity" in school attendance can be "particularly beneficial."[15] This finding suggests that scheduling practices at private vocational schools, in addition to other benefits, may also have a positive effect upon many students' learning experiences.

From the standpoint of the vocational schools, the principal incentive for year-round operations is, of course, the need to utilize buildings, equipment and staff as fully as possible. Many schools, therefore, close for vacation only two weeks during the year (the Christmas season and one week in July). It is at these times that instructors take their vacations.

Day or Evening Classes

Students generally have the option of attending school on a day or evening basis. Daytime attendance, often with a choice of mornings

[15] *The New York Times*, April 7, 1968, p. E-9.

or afternoons, is preferred by the majority of students; and the median division for the 128 schools is about 75 percent daytime and 25 percent evening enrollments. Only 20 schools (or 16 percent of the total) limit their classes to the daytime; a single school offers only evening classes. Otherwise, arrangements vary widely. Fifteen schools enroll 60 percent of their students during the day and 40 percent in the evening; 80 percent day enrollment and 20 percent evening enrollment was the next most common arrangement, and obtained in 12 schools.

A school owner in New York City is convinced that the peak enrollments that had once been attained in evening sessions were unlikely ever to be matched again. He reasoned that there is a decreasing number of persons with the ambition to work full-time and also attend evening classes. Another school president, who also franchises five schools, believes that there is considerable capacity in many schools for enrolling students in afternoon sessions. Students, however, seem to prefer morning classes; moreover, some employers apparently are unable or unwilling to adjust work shifts so that students employed at their firms could attend school in the afternoon.

Full- or Part-Time Classes
and Course Lengths

There is an exact correlation in most of the schools between day and evening enrollments and full- and part-time enrollments. A school with 60 percent day attendance and 40 percent evening attendance would usually have the same percentages attending on full- and part-time bases. But enrollments in more than one-fourth of the schools do not coincide in this way. At times, as shown below for a school in Illinois, the differences are substantial.

Percent of students enrolled days	43%
Percent of students enrolled evenings	57
Percent of students enrolled full-time	78
Percent of students enrolled part-time	22

The combination of courses varying greatly in length plus the option of enrolling in a course on either a full- or part-time basis affords considerable flexibility to students. Three hundred eighty-eight courses at reporting NATTS schools range in length from half a week to 130 weeks. The median for these courses was 40 weeks.[16]

Most, but not all, of the full-time courses are also offered on a part-time basis; and a much smaller number of courses are available only

[16] The mode, for all full-time courses, was 18 weeks (in 24 schools); the next most frequent period was 52 weeks in 23 schools.

on a part-time basis. More than 300 part-time courses ranged from 1.5 to 225 weeks in length. The median was 71 weeks, or nearly double the median for full-time courses; and, as reported in the NATTS Directory of member schools, most part-time courses are about twice the length of full-time courses.

The following example illustrates the variety of schedules open to a student enrolling in a *die design* course:

Course Length in Weeks[17]

Full-Time	Part-Time
48	96/144

This means that a student attending full-time during the day would be expected to complete the course in 48 weeks, whereas a student attending evenings or part-time would be expected to complete the course in either 96 or 144 weeks. The evening students who finish in 96 weeks attend classes Monday, Wednesday and Friday evenings, and sometimes even Saturdays; the students completing the course in 144 weeks would probably have classes Tuesday and Thursday evenings.

It should also be explained that course lengths listed in a school's catalog are often only typical or "average." Students in most courses can graduate at different time intervals, depending on their individual achievement. Also, as noted in a later chapter, many schools do permit students to repeat part of or even an entire course, and this is usually at no additional tuition.

Flexible Operations: School Profitability and Employer Needs

The economic relationships between private vocational schools and the private enterprise sector are intimate and mutually advantageous. Many employers have found that the schools can expeditiously accommodate their need for trained personnel. In exchange, the schools are continuously apprised of changes that should be adopted in training programs. They also build up a list of potential employers for their graduates.

Employer Acceptance of Private Schools

Initially, some employers felt that a school was not the ideal setting or means for occupational training. This position has been reversed in

[17] This represents the course scheduling at one school; it could differ at another school.

many industries, which no longer maintain that the novice must learn on the job. The private vocational schools have gained greater acceptance because of their demonstrated skills in training. The state directors of education who oversee private vocational schools can also be credited with correcting the schools' unfavorable image. These officials, found in only about 20 of the states, have helped to modify the once prevailing view that private vocational schools were disreputable — a generalization often based upon the undesirable practices of only a minority of the schools.[18] Moreover, as new courses evolve (and this has been a notable feature of proprietary schools), these schools may have increasing opportunities for supplying the public sector with persons trained in a variety of service occupations. The positions could include: child care specialist, forest ranger, geriatric aide, home health aide, landscaping aide, nurse aide, recreation aide, traffic manager and water pollution control aide.

Despite recent gains in private vocational education, the medical profession, at least through some of its associations, has still insisted that 1) technicians and aides attend a college or university for two years, or 2) profit-making schools cannot perform a genuine service. However, even these views are apparently being examined and slowly revised. And in any case, this opposition has not proved entirely detrimental to the schools since doctors and hospital administrators have continued to fill acute occupational shortages with graduates of private technical schools.

Mutuality of Interests

The private schools and employers have mutual interests. With the exception of the growing number of schools owned and operated by corporations, there is minimal competition between the two.[19]

In most occupational areas where goods or services are produced as a result of the training, sales are not executed with either consumers or business firms. There are of course exceptions, such as schools of barbering, cosmetology, automobile repair and cooking. However, even in these cases the consumers are often persons who cannot afford many basic necessities, including the price of a haircut in a regular barber

[18] Even in 1967, the president of a technical school in Milwaukee remarked: ". . . the failure or dishonesty of one school reflects on all of us."

[19] Private vocational schools and unions have generally not been competitors either. In many of the apprenticeable crafts (e.g., construction) where the unions are active in implementing on-the-job training, the private schools simply do not provide training. In the comparatively few instances where unions have operated schools they have often been actuated by the failure of public schools to keep pace with changes in an occupation's requirements. The unions in the food preparation industry have provided at least one major school with money to publish a cookbook for students.

shop. A recent exception is the practice instituted at some of the schools offering courses in computer operations and programming. At least one business school has been renting the use of its costly equipment (when not in use by students) to business and professional organizations. Were it not for this innovation, student tuition would have become "prohibitively high." "The additional effect is to keep the school staff in touch with developments in the world outside the classroom," according to the Executive Director of the United Business Schools Association.[20]

Other private schools donate items to charitable or non-profit organizations. The Culinary Institute of America caters the Harvard-Yale football games in New Haven only because there is no local caterer equipped to service such a large number of spectators.

Subcontracting of Training by Business Firms

In addition, a growing number of employers are deciding that it is desirable (and even preferable) to have at least some workers who are trained in schools rather than on the job; this can also benefit the worker who is anxious to progress rapidly in his occupation. For instance, journeymen mechanics and master chefs are often extremely busy or else their time is considered too valuable to allocate much of it for training apprentices. Small firms, offices, or stores have often relied upon private vocational schools for the training of their work force. Their limited financial capabilities have precluded training on the job and employees were expected to self-finance their schooling.[21]

Although figures are unavailable, it is likely that many larger business and industrial concerns have become convinced that at least the good schools can provide more than entry-level training for their workers; and therefore it is more efficient to subcontract training requirements to private schools rather than train on the job.[22]

Benefits of School-Industry Cooperation

Once a school has established a good reputation with the employers in the industry(ies) it serves, the direct and informal contacts prove

[20] Richard Fulton, "Proprietary Schools," a forthcoming article in *Encyclopedia of Educational Research*, Fourth Edition.

[21] Alice M. Rivlin, "Critical Issues in the Development of Vocational Education," in *Unemployment in a Prosperous Economy*, A Report of the Princeton Manpower Symposium, May 13–14, 1965, edited by William G. Bowen and Frederick M. Harbison (Princeton, N.J.: Princeton University Industrial Relations Section, 1965), p. 163.

[22] Subcontracting for building maintenance and other services has become increasingly common within recent years.

very beneficial.[23] The useful employer arrangements established by private schools are especially meaningful in view of the fact that the *organized* advisory committees to public vocational schools, composed of industrial and business leaders, have not been uniformly notable for their success in recommending changes.[24]

Continuing discussions between private school administrators and managers of enterprises can result in rapid modifications of instructional programs. Meetings may even take place in the schools, as, for instance, when acute shortages of truck drivers impelled truck owners to visit a school and "give all sorts of suggestions." The President of Lincoln Technical Institute in Newark, New Jersey, pointed out in testimony before a Congressional subcommittee that his school had made immediate adjustments in service and repair courses when serious social problems were recognized:

1) During the Northeast's severe water shortage, summer of 1966, the prohibition on the use of water-cooled air conditioners necessitated conversion of that equipment to an air-cooled type.

2) The 1968 model automobiles contained an emission control device to diminish air pollution.

3) The New York Metropolitan Area's concern over air pollution was expressed in legislation that led the school ". . . to include additional instruction on oil fired heating equipment with respect to its possible contribution to air pollution."[25]

During these Congressional hearings, the President of Midway Technical Institute of Chicago testified that a boat manufacturer had asked him to set up a course in the repair of fiberglass boats.[26]

Businesslike Behavior of Private Schools

The functions of private vocational schools have certainly been influenced by 1) the fact that most of the schools are proprietary, and

[23] Career Academy, located in Milwaukee and several other cities, is a prime example of the growing regard for private vocational schools. This technical school (which is admittedly unique) was listed on the American Stock Exchange in 1967 after an underwriting of $9 million. According to a school owner, "Ten years ago, Wall Street would not have touched a proprietary school."

[24] See Samuel M. Burt, *Industry and Vocational-Technical Education* (New York: McGraw-Hill Book Company, 1967), for a discussion of effective advisory committees.

[25] J. Warren Davies, prepared statement in U. S. Congress, House Committee on Education and Labor, *Partnership for Learning and Earning Act of 1968,* Hearings before the General Subcommittee on Education of the Committee on Education and Labor, House of Representatives, on HR 15066, 90th Congress, Second Session, 1968, p. 350.

[26] One school, in a more formal relationship, has a Professional Advisory Committee that consists of visiting dentists and surgeons.

2) their establishment of close working relations with profit-seeking enterprises. As a result, the schools have both adopted and adapted many of the operations found among business firms.[27] It has, however, never been a one-sided exchange since numerous concerns have used the schools as a substitute for at least some of their training activities. Certain industrial establishments have, as noted, absorbed schools and operate them as thriving subdivisions.

Private schools generally find it advantageous to incorporate when their enrollments become comparatively large. It will be recalled that the members of NATTS (comprising a small minority of all trade and technical schools) were on the average considerably larger than the nonmember schools. The percentage frequency distribution below shows that 80 percent of the 128 reporting NATTS schools were organized as business corporations. Another 8 percent of the member schools were nonprofit organizations and some of them were presumably large

business corporation	79.7%
single ownership	10.9
partnership	1.6
nonprofit corporation approved by the Internal Revenue Service	7.8
	100%

enough to benefit taxwise thereby. Whereas less than 15 percent of trade and technical schools were organized as a single ownership or partnership, nearly three times that percentage of surveyed business schools had the same forms of organization.[28] As the membership of NATTS grows, corporate ownership will undoubtedly begin to resemble more closely that of UBSA.

Interest in Operating at Full Capacity

In view of their concern for maximizing profits, the private vocational schools naturally attempt to achieve enrollments that approach full capacity. Presumably many of the schools succeed; and, according to an administrator of the private schools in a large state, this is

[27] The ability of a school to continue its operations under extremely challenging circumstances was demonstrated by RCA Institutes when it held regular classes on a Friday evening and then moved all its equipment in 150 vans to a new site in time to resume classes Monday morning at 8 o'clock. See *The New York Times*, Jan. 15, 1968, p. 44.

[28] The business school information is based upon a survey conducted by the UBSA to which 263 member schools responded.

a principal reason why the proprietary schools are considerably less costly to operate than the public schools.

Before considering the potential capacity for all trade and technical schools, the small minority of schools which do not operate during the summer months should be mentioned. Certain of these schools do not offer a summer program in order to accommodate the students who are required to work full-time for several months of the year. Even some of these schools may maximally utilize their facilities for novel purposes. As an example, the Culinary Institute of America (CIA), a nonprofit institution, has offered a two-week refresher course in professional cooking for competent cooks, restaurateurs, and food supervisors. More recently, the school began offering a teacher training course in the culinary field.[29] Potential candidates were sought among:

1) Chefs and experienced food service personnel who needed training in teaching methods;
2) Experienced teachers who needed intensive training in the culinary arts;
3) Mature, qualified applicants who may have had some background and experience in either or both areas (culinary and educational), but who needed further training in either or both;
4) Retired military food service personnel.[30]

The Director of the CIA has indicated that he would really prefer to utilize any excess capacity at the school — either during the regular school term or in the summer months — for training programs directed at welfare recipients, persons with criminal records and other problem students. Faculty members, too, expressed a preference for such challenges over their present "moonlighting" as chefs.[31] Such a program, it was claimed, could be financed under the Manpower Development and Training Act; and the staff would also provide remedial work.

The belief that extra income would not be worth the effort was the principal reason cited by schools not wishing to increase capacity; and they probably deliberated in the same way that any other business firm would, trying to evaluate expected costs and benefits. (Upper limits on expansion are sometimes imposed by a school's need to pro-

[29] The Institute had received a contract to upgrade and amplify the knowledge of home economics teachers who were brought to New Haven under a public utility's sponsorship.

[30] *Alumni News,* Alumni of the Culinary Institute of America (New Haven, Connecticut, Nov. 15, 1967).

[31] The Director related that a trainee's eyes light up when a visitor (e.g., the mayor) shows that he is enjoying the food.

vide practical training on large and expensive equipment.) The remaining schools that responded negatively referred about equally to the competition of public schools and a shortage of instructors.

On the basis of responses to the questionnaire appearing in Appendix II, 85 percent of the 128 responding NATTS member schools, which generally operate on a year-round basis, would be interested in expanding the size of their student enrollment. According to the responses of NATTS members, plus the estimates of observers of proprietary education, the potential for enrollment expansion among trade and technical schools (and also barbering, business and cosmetology) are probably immense.[32] Only a minority of schools that offer day and evening sessions operate near capacity in their afternoon classes. This is probably a major reason why the NATTS schools indicated that their capacity enrollment was approximately 100,000. Since the actual number of students attending the schools in 1966 was about 60,000, it would appear that these schools were operating at only 60 percent of their capacity. If this average rate of operations were applied to all trade and technical schools (estimated to number 3,000), the potential expansion in enrollment can be figured at more than ½ million students.

Student Referrals and Recruitment

The private schools utilize two principal sources for new students: the referrals of enrolled students or graduates[33] and active recruitment by paid representatives of the schools.

Student referrals are useful on two counts: 1) they are a significant index of student satisfaction;[34] and 2) they enable the school to save the fee that would normally be paid for newspaper advertising or to a sales representative.[35] Moreover, it is usually the more competent students who will recommend a private vocational school to their friends and relatives.

Several school presidents were convinced that because of the competitive pressure from other schools, nearly every school needs sales representatives to recruit students. A school has the option of relying

[32] Undoubtedly, many school owners would expand when the opportunity arose, or, as a number of school owners put it, ". . . whenever the enrollment warrants it."

[33] Employer referrals are usually a less important source for new students.

[34] An unknown number of schools pay their current students up to $10, or give a gift for bringing a new student into the school.

[35] To the extent that a school's representatives successfully screen applicants, they may reduce the costs of interviewing prospective applicants.

upon its own staff for recruitment or contracting with persons outside the school who perform the specialized service. The outside sales representative is usually paid on a commission basis and is occasionally employed by several different schools. His leads come from newspaper and mail advertising paid for by the trade or technical school.

Several advantages seem to inhere in using regular employees to recruit students. In the first place, they are unlikely to exaggerate the value of a school's program because they are not motivated primarily by the desire for a commission. Secondly, when a school's permanent representative is considered acceptable by a high school and its guidance counselors, he is invited to discuss the opportunities of private vocational schooling at annual career day programs. Of course, not all schools, even within the same state, extend a welcome to the representatives of proprietary schools.

Conscientious and honest school administrators are naturally concerned with preventing the indiscretions or malpractice of some outside representatives. One student claimed that the salesman who had visited his home had exaggerated somewhat when he said a course did not require much mathematics. A school administrator in Washington, D.C., described some of the representatives at their worst as follows: "These fellows are as itinerant as the fly-by-night schools. Sometimes there is a group movement [school and sales representative]; they literally swamp one area and then move on to another area, almost like a circus." This extreme situation is naturally directly related to the nature and operation of a school and can be avoided by schools that are permanently based in a community. One school, which may have had some unfortunate experiences, requires that its representatives have listed telephone numbers and be residents of an area for a couple of years.

Even the many good schools must carefully regulate the practices of their representatives. This is most effectively accomplished by giving a representative authority to bring a student to a school only as a potential enrollee; he is not allowed to pass upon the student's final acceptance. This arrangement tends to lead to fewer rejections, because a representative will strive to select students who fit a school's requirements.

An advisor to several proprietary schools addressed the 1967 Annual Convention of NATTS and listed the following multiple responsibilities that flow from the initial contact with a prospective student: "An inquiry is no good unless it leads to a student; but a student is no good unless he becomes a graduate; and a graduate is no good unless he is placed in a job, and if necessary, continues to be placed." This implies that representatives must be highly selective.[36] They should not merely be wooed by the $50 to $60 they receive from some schools for each student who registers for a course.[37] In short, although representatives are often hired because of their demonstrated sales ability, they must be convinced that *all* students should not necessarily be sold on a course or even a school.

The inspection members of the NATTS Accrediting Commission devote considerable attention to the practices as well as the forms of a school's representatives. For example, at least two schools were told to stop using the word "counselors" in lieu of sales representatives. A keen member of a visiting inspection team advised one school that its sales representative receive one-half of his commission when he signs up a student and the other half only when the student is enrolled. But the school indicated that representatives "live from hand to mouth and need total payment as soon as possible."

When it was suggested that greater recognition of the schools might eliminate (or at least reduce) the number of outside representatives and thereby make it possible to reduce tuition costs, objections were raised. The first dealt with the common use of representatives by most colleges. (In reality, probably only a small minority of the college representatives are paid on a commission basis and, in any case, they would invariably be on the college payroll.[38]) Private vocational schools would therefore still require someone to publicize the objectives of their training in order to compete with the colleges. The administrator of a school that trains hotel-motel personnel gave another reason for maintaining at least some representatives — namely, the need to inform older persons of the opportunities available for a second career.

Schools on Wheels

Mobile and "term" schools are additional examples of the flexibility and ingenuity of proprietary vocational schools. Such schools illustrate the attempts to extend recruitment geographically by making facilities

[36] At times of course a school may advise its representatives to lower the usual admission requirements in order to enroll an applicant. As discussed later, however, this may be a sensible, pragmatic and honest procedure if a school offers a variety of course levels, or graduates its students in the same course at *different* levels of proficiency.

[37] Some schools were known to give $25 to their representatives for each aptitude test administered in a prospective student's home. This was considered unfortunate by several school owners, who felt that representatives could become primarily concerned with garnering the $25 rather than with choosing wisely among potential applicants.

[38] A business school owner, who also franchises other schools, claimed that community and junior colleges in Miami use the same advertising techniques as the private schools.

available to students located in a community that often cannot support a school. If any distinction can be made between these two types of schools, it is that the mobile schools are geared to move from one community to another, spending a few weeks or months on each site. The term schools are similar, but they may plan, or hope, to remain permanently in some of the communities they visit.

The mobile schools may either make regular visits to communities throughout a state, or rent space in a community that experiences a sudden upsurge in the need for trained persons. One mobile school, specializing in dental technician training, made regular visits to several communities in the State of Washington. The other type of service occurs when, for instance, a large employer decides to establish a manufacturing plant in a medium-size community that has a low unemployment rate, but may be adjacent to a rural area with underemployed people.

Other schools, however, have arrived in a town and used highly effective promotional campaigns that often oversold the advantages of their training programs. Such fly-by-night organizations have proven elusive because they often move before a state's regulatory body is even aware of their presence, or before any evidence of malpractice can be established by a Better Business Bureau.

Term schools were rather common at one time.[39] They operated as follows: officials of a proprietary school entered a city with a population of 30,000 to 50,000 and met with Chamber of Commerce personnel, industrial leaders and local government officials. They described the operation of the school over a specific time period as well as their previous successes in other cities. The community leaders saw, at times, the possibility of a school's remaining in the community on a permanent basis if it prospered, and this naturally engendered more interest. Representatives of a local bank were often called in (if they were not already present for discussions), and the bank often agreed to finance tuition payments; this involved setting up installments, and the school, therefore, assumed only a small risk. Some of the students were financed by local business and industrial firms.

Most of the mobile or term schools were generally found in sections of the South, the Midwest and the Far West, with few urban centers and numerous sparsely settled communities. On the other hand, the Elkins Institute of Radio and Electronics in Dallas has operated term schools to train employees of the Bell System companies for FCC

[39] The Massey Institute of Jacksonville, which functioned throughout the state of Florida, utilized a cattle truck for moving furniture and blackboards; they also had a contract with a typewriter dealer for placing machines in communities where they might be needed.

licenses; and the Lincoln Technical Institute in Newark has run term schools for oil heat dealers and garage owners' associations.

There are undoubtedly still many places (e.g., urban ghettos) where prospective students are highly immobile and could benefit from some form of mobile school. An outstanding example of such an accommodation occurred when the Electronic Computer Programming Institute (ECPI) trained several inmates at Sing Sing Prison in Ossining, New York, as computer programmers. The project was considered so successful that 20 additional inmates were enrolled in May 1968 and the course became a permanent part of the prison's rehabilitation program.

Multiple Ownership and Franchising of Schools

Multiple school ownership and issuance of franchises by individual schools offer some indication of the profitable and growing opportunities in vocational training. This potential is given further credence by the increased ownership of proprietary schools by many well-established industrial firms.

The frequency of multiple ownership and franchising was demonstrated in the responses of 128 schools affiliated with NATTS. Seventy-eight of the schools could be classified as independent because they had no affiliation with any other school or industrial concern. The remaining 50 schools (about 40 percent of all respondents) included 20 branch schools that were owned or franchised, and 30 parent schools that were owners or franchisers. The 30 parent schools reported owning 93 schools and franchising 20 schools — i.e., the 30 parent schools had some control over 113 others; and about 70 percent of the branch schools were located in a state different from that of the parent school.

Although the maximum number of schools franchised by a single reporting NATTS school was only seven, there are several sizable franchisers among the trade, technical and business schools. These schools or organizations can naturally exert an important influence on the operations and programs of the independent schools.

The Electronic Computer Programming Institute in New York City has been in business for 12 years and is one of the oldest schools in its field. ECPI operates three schools directly for the principal purposes of "control and research"; the income from these schools, according to the management, is a secondary goal. In 1967 the number of students in all their franchised schools totaled 28,500.[40] By April 1968, ECPI had franchised more than 90 schools in the United States, two in London and one in Canada, and it anticipated having

[40] "The Teaching Business," *Barron's*, April 8, 1968, p. 11.

110 schools by the end of 1968. Relatively tight controls are imposed upon the franchisees in exchange for information on new instructional techniques that are tested and proven at the schools owned by ECPI.[41]

About 500 business schools in the United States and abroad have a rather distinctive franchise in Speedwriting (a form of shorthand) and Nancy Taylor programs. Unlike many other franchises, there is no management fee or guarantee of territory. The extent of franchising between franchiser and schools consists mainly of the sale of course books to the schools, who in turn sell them to their students. The schools do receive other services, including instruction on setting up taped dictation laboratories, free teacher training (in New York or regionally), and the support of national advertising. A salient flexibility, from the viewpoint of students, permits easy transfer from one school to another, and every graduate of a Speedwriting course can attend any school in the country for purposes of brush-up.

The promising overall opportunities in proprietary training have been hailed as follows: "A new dimension may be on the horizon, as large publicly-held corporations are beginning to purchase business and technical schools which will be operated as subsidiaries." A Bank of America study has shown "that a properly run proprietary school can be a sound investment."[42] Presumably companies that acquire private schools compare their profitability with other investments. A decision to purchase a school suggests a conviction that the need for training is and will continue to be great; and it may also imply that public schools will not be able to offer certain types of training or else they simply will not expand enough to meet all training requirements.

Table 3–7 contains a partial list of corporation-owned vocational schools and available information on the number and location of the schools.[43] The 11 corporations own at least 67 schools in the United States and abroad.[44] Other corporations own schools generally limited to purchasers of their equipment. The International Business Machines Corporation confines attendance in its non-tuition schools to users of their computer equipment. The Bear Manufacturing Company of Rock Island, Illinois, also operates an automotive safety service school, which is mainly, but not exclusively, for "owners or

[41] "The company makes little money on the initial $20,000 investment by franchisees, which about covers pre-opening costs; the 6% royalty charge against their gross revenues, however, is virtually clear profit." *Ibid.*, p. 15.

[42] Richard Fulton, "Proprietary Schools," *loc. cit.*

[43] The Bell and Howell Corporation has announced that it will add more than 30 additional Institutes and include several new courses.

[44] Besides several of the publicly-held companies listed in Table 3–7, the following independent schools have securities traded on stock exchanges: ECPI and Computer Education, Inc., one of its franchises; Programming & Systems, Inc.; and Career Academy, Inc. See *Barron's*, April 8, 1968, p. 11.

TABLE 3-7

PARTIAL LIST OF CORPORATION-OWNED VOCATIONAL SCHOOLS

Company	Available Information on Schools Owned	No. of Schools
Bell and Howell Corp.	DeVry Institute of Technology, Chicago DeVry Institute of Technology, Phoenix DeVry Institute of Technology, Toronto, Can.	3
Computing and Software, Inc.	14 West Coast trade schools in Southern California International Tabulating Institute, Washington, D.C.	14 1
Control Data Corp.	Control Data Institutes in Atlanta; Arlington, Va.; Boston; Dallas; Detroit; Miami; Minneapolis; New York; St. Louis; Los Angeles, and Frankfurt, Germany	11
The Foxboro Co.	The New England School of Art	1
International Telephone and Telegraph Corp.	Allied Institute of Technology, Chicago Bailey Technical School, St. Louis ITT Business Institute, Evansville, Ind. ITT Technical Institute, Dayton, Ohio Massachusetts Trades Shops School, Boston Sams Technical Institute, Evansville, Ind. Sams Technical Institute, Fort Wayne, Ind. Sams Technical Institute, Indianapolis, Ind. The Speedwriting Co., New York	9
International Textbook Co.[a]	Institute of Computer Science	1
Lear Siegler Corp.	10 schools offering computer programming and business courses and 4 schools offering only computer programming	14
Litton Industries	7 institutes of computer management	7
McGraw-Hill Corp.	Capitol Radio Engineering Institute, Washington, D.C.	1
Philco Corporation (Div.) of Ford Motor Corp.	3 schools (in Philadelphia, Palo Alto and Thailand)	3
Radio Corp. of America	RCA Institutes, New York, N.Y. RCA Institutes, Cherry Hill, N.J.	2
TOTALS: Companies: 11	Schools:	67

[a] This company also owns International Correspondence Schools, which has enrolled more than 100,000 students during each of the past five years.

operators of Bear equipment"; and some previous work experience is required.[45] The National Institute of Drycleaning in Silver Spring, Maryland, is the international trade association for more than 8,000 member plants; the school it operates is open to both members and nonmembers.

Corporations have acquired vocational schools for reasons that extend beyond a directly defined interest in maximizing profits. For instance,

[45] "Training the Automotive Specialist at Bear," Rock Island, Illinois. (Bulletin.)

one concern plans to train a large number of South Americans in automobile mechanics for a car-rental division of the company. Another company plans to offer scholarships to its employees and provide courses in its school that are attuned to the company's needs.

The extent of a company's involvement in the functioning of acquired vocational schools varies greatly, but a school's curricula are likely to reflect trade and technical changes when the field of production of the parent company coincides with the acquired school's training. The director of one school, which is now a subsidiary of a large manufacturer, believes that the private schools are going through a process similar to that of many nursing homes — i.e., just as nursing homes were taken over from nurses who once operated them, so the private schools are being purchased by industrial and business firms which also establish fiscal and training standards. It is really doubtful that most companies will, however, become any more involved in the operation of their schools than they have in other business mergers that have been effected. In one known case, a corporation expects its schools to "make it on their own"; this includes payment for equipment that the company manufactures and the school uses. Moreover, only about five percent of the school's graduates are hired by the parent firm. In contrast, another large concern charges its schools no more than cost price for very expensive manufactured equipment.[46]

[46] This may seem, to many economic theorists, inconsistent with the most efficient allocation of a company's resources. However, some firms have argued that careful attempts at costing are not worth the effort.

CHAPTER 4

Evaluation: An Outstanding Need

"[Accreditation] provides the school with an objective method to up-grade educational standards and practices, and externally it assists prospective students and practicing guidance counselors with a professional institutional evaluation."

— RICHARD FULTON, Executive Director and
General Counsel,
United Business
Schools Association

The ultimate value of private vocational schools depends upon the graduates' success in finding training-related positions, and their occupational advancement during their working careers.

Chapter 9 includes some student evaluations of the relevance of the training they had received in private trade schools to their jobs, as well as the satisfaction with the jobs and their rates of progress. However, this follow-up was limited to a period of 18 months after leaving vocational school.[1]

An exhaustive evaluation of private schools could involve educators and economists in a comparison of the employment progress of students trained in private vocational schools, public vocational schools and on-the-job programs. Although such a broad-gauged study (also including comparison of costs) could be instructive, it would naturally not be conclusive or binding for all time. Schools and other training organizations change their curricula and instructional staffs; and some schools simply lag by failing to adopt the changes instituted by other schools. Therefore some continuing means must be devised to evaluate any training institution, including proprietary vocational schools.

This chapter outlines some of the evaluation methods adopted by private and public agencies concerned with the operating standards of private vocational schools. The approach is often practical and this

---

[1] Employer evaluation of private school graduates would be relevant, too, but such a survey was not made.

seems appropriate. Instruction in these schools is, after all, provided in a concrete setting that frequently simulates work sites in shops or laboratories; and the schools explicitly state an occupational goal for each training program.

A school can best serve its long-range interest by encouraging comment and even criticism from a maximum number of sources. This is an important reason why schools maintain contact with their graduates. It was also the principal stimulus for the establishment of an association of trade and technical schools by a few school owners in 1965. Although the proprietary schools have been (and still are) highly individualistic, farsighted school owners realized that an organization such as NATTS could improve the reputation and opportunities of all *effective* schools.

Accreditation

Accreditation refers to the process of evaluating a school on the basis of its success in achieving the purposes and objectives the school has set for itself. This process does not exhaustively assess the employment prospects for graduates of any particular training course; this responsibility rests more appropriately with others, including, for instance, competent job counselors. However, the demands of employers for persons trained in specific occupations are signals to which a school must respond if it is concerned in the long run with maintaining high student enrollment.[2]

In contrast to policies governing private schools in other countries, their accreditation in the United States has been conducted largely through voluntary, nongovernmental organizations.[3] The voluntary nature of the system presupposes that accreditation is in the best interests of both students and schools. As referred to again later, a school's claims concerning its courses or programs are verified principally by technical specialists (industry representatives and school owners) who are not affiliated with the particular school. Therefore, competition in either course format or tuition is not diminished. In fact, the suggestions offered by the outside accrediting team should both increase competition and improve instructional quality.

Until August 1967, proprietary trade and technical schools had no formal means of being evaluated, since less than half of all states license the operations of proprietary schools and a much smaller percentage of the states carefully supervise the instructional programs

[2] Schools with low standards and certainly those with only short-term profit objectives would be unlikely to apply for accreditation, although even many good private vocational schools have not yet applied for accreditation.

[3] Publicly financed programs do require that certain standards be met, including at times accreditation by a private organization.

offered by the schools.[4] Even in New York, though a school must be in business for two years before it can qualify for a license, new schools (including those with programming courses) can operate on an unlicensed basis.

In 1967 the U. S. Office of Education designated NATTS a nationally recognized agency of accreditation for trade and technical schools after a variety of organizational representatives — including guidance counselors, industrial authorities, educators and others — were satisfied that NATTS could effectively accredit its schools. Shortly after NATTS received its designation from the U. S. Office of Education, nearly 100 schools applied for membership in the Association, which is now granted only after a school has been accredited. Requests for information were received from hundreds of other schools.

Besides the practical benefits of accreditation — including outside evaluation and suggested improvements in a school's functioning — accreditation focuses attention on competent schools and enhances their competitive status with counselors and prospective students; and the poor schools may be compelled to improve their teaching standards, purchase required equipment and, in general, raise their capital base.[5]

Some owners have maintained legitimate schools in one location and questionable schools in other areas. Presumably, this has occurred in the absence of effective regulation by public or private organizations in certain states. In the past, the reputable schools were damaged by the excesses of these poorly operated schools, and they welcomed the raising of standards. One school administrator remarked: "We already have a nice share of the market and under more ideal conditions, we would welcome the *worry* of competing schools."

Schools accredited by NATTS will now be favored under certain government programs and this further enhances the position of the better schools. For instance, students at most proprietary schools could not qualify for loans under the National Vocational Student Loan Insurance Act until the U. S. Office of Education designated NATTS a nationally recognized agency of accreditation.

Finally, an accrediting body includes persons who are familiar with current changes in industry, and hence qualified to evaluate occupational training. This is especially important when new jobs arise for which work standards and practices are not yet firmly established.

The numerous occupations recently generated by the rapidly grow-

[4] The Accrediting Commission for Business Schools and the National Home Study Council had been designated by the U. S. Commisioner of Education as nationally recognized accrediting associations before 1967.

[5] Some poorly financed schools have failed and left their students stranded with little legal recourse.

ing computer industry are a prime example. Data processing and computer programming courses became available in about 700 schools, within a three-year period and problems arose.

Bleats about advertising claims and charges of deceptive practices have been reaching Better Business Bureaus and local and state agencies. Indeed, the Federal Trade Commission has required one school in the Midwest to stop promising jobs with IBM to its graduates.[6]

Although NATTS and UBSA have thus far accredited only about 30 schools with programming courses, their by-laws are comprehensive. A NATTS member school must seek accreditation for any newly acquired affiliate. In addition, when an accredited school launches a new course it must submit detailed information on the course to the NATTS Accrediting Commission; if the course is unrelated to those that formed the previous basis for accreditation, the new course must be independently accredited.[7]

Multiple Accreditation and Competition Among Accrediting Agencies

Some schools offer courses in a variety of occupations but this has not led (at least yet) to problems of multiple accreditation. For example, the Federal Aviation Agency (FAA) rules on the *safety* features of the training at flight schools but does not accredit the schools; therefore the FAA does not really compete with NATTS. Also, although both NATTS and the Committee on Engineering Technology of the Engineers' Council for Professional Development accredit schools that train technicians, the latter limits its purview to schools offering a two-year course and meeting other requirements for the training of engineering technicians. Many schools offer both trade and business courses; and programming is taught at trade, technical and business schools, but these situations have not necessarily led to serious conflicts.

In at least one case, the American Dental Association (ADA) and NATTS have reached a promising accord. The ADA has different rules from NATTS for accrediting non-professional dental personnel. The ADA's course length requirements are often higher than those of NATTS; moreover ADA's by-laws do not permit it to consider applications for accreditation from proprietary schools. But the Association has still agreed that when it receives inquiries from schools not eligible for ADA accreditation, it will indicate that the school can have "access

---

[6] "How Good Are Computer Schools?" *Business Week*, October 7, 1967, p. 97.

[7] Unfortunately, newly formed and unaffiliated schools interested only in the maximization of immediate profits are still comparatively free to operate unhindered within many states.

to NATTS accreditation" (if that happens to be the case). NATTS is hopeful of achieving similar cooperation with other professional organizations.[8]

Another major goal of many NATTS members is the formulation of one standard definition of qualified private training institutions that would be acceptable to public agencies. For instance, states may accept NATTS accreditation for students financed under the "Cold War G.I. Bill" but do not have to do so; on the other hand, NATTS accreditation is consistently acceptable under the National Vocational Student Loan Insurance Act.

State Licensing and Regulation[9]

State licensing of proprietary occupational schools is only found in about 20 states and the regulations vary widely.[10] The major concerns of these states include: financial soundness (e.g., requirement to post bond), qualifications of teachers, course outlines, adequacy of equipment, contracts with students and advertising claims.

In general, the inspection of private schools by most state supervisors is not as thorough as that of a NATTS accrediting team. State supervisors often have an exceptionally heavy work load. Even in New York one supervisor may oversee about 50 schools, and he is expected to visit each school about three times annually; in some large states one supervisor is responsible for visiting all schools. A state supervisor, moreover, is often compelled to devote many hours to a school's special problems ("emergencies"), giving him less time for other important matters. In contrast, a NATTS accrediting team is composed of industry specialists in every subject offered at a school, who evaluate the teaching in each course. New York and possibly a few other states utilize subject specialists only when a school begins teaching a new course. According to a New York law, each course

---

[8] A magazine published by the American Medical Association referred to private trade and technical schools as one of the sources for paramedical training. See Ralph Bugg, "When College Isn't the Answer," *Today's Health*, Vol. 46, No. 8, August 1968, p. 42.

[9] For a more detailed discussion, see Chapter 3 of Harold F. Clark and Harold S. Sloan, *Classrooms on Main Street* (New York: Columbia University Teachers College Press, 1966).

[10] "Licensing is nothing more than a permit to do business, having regard generally to safety and commercial standards. Certification, on the other hand, is generally related to curriculum, instructional staff, facilities, etc. . . ." See Richard Fulton, "Proprietary Schools," a forthcoming article in *Encyclopedia of Educational Research*, Fourth Edition.

The term *certification* is not introduced in this chapter, but it is generally clear when there is reference to it.

must be re-evaluated every five years; this coincides with the *maximum* period required of NATTS schools.

The state supervisors, even in New York, are not responsible for the range of schools dealt with by the private associations. This may simply be due to the regulatory opinions of state legislators. Hence, in New York, schools of business, data processing, baby nursing and many newly introduced courses are exempt from licensing, although the schools may voluntarily apply for it. But the state may be more exacting with regard to the formal preparation required of instructors. In New York, for example, the instructors must enroll in teacher-training courses unless they are professionals — that is, certified teachers, doctors, dentists, engineers, etc.[11] NATTS, on the other hand, is primarily concerned with whether the teachers keep up with current changes in their trade; and it expects them to attend meetings as members of their trade associations.

As a general recommendation, it would be desirable for states to license proprietary vocational schools in their states, and for accreditation to be continued voluntarily by a private organization. Supervision should be adopted by all states, and supervisory staffs must of course be adequately supported. State supervisors could perhaps devote most of their attention to the schools that are unaccredited. If feasible, state supervisors and a private accrediting group such as NATTS could alternate in their inspections of schools say, every two and a half years.[12]

Some school owners are convinced that states should do more than merely license and regulate private schools. The stability and growth of private schools should be encouraged, they urge, because the schools are prime sources for occupational training as a result of their capacity to innovate and operate flexibly; various professional services, therefore, should also be provided by the state. The careful interpre-

[11] In New York new teachers must have two years of high school and five years experience as a journeyman to qualify for a temporary license. A teacher-training course of 30 hours is offered by the State Education Department and it must be taken within a year. Another teacher-training course of 30 hours must be taken every three years to renew the license.

[12] Mr. Boyd A. Finch, Director, Vocational Standards Section, Division of Vocational Education for the State of Arkansas, presents a valid position in the following excerpt from a letter dated March 5, 1968:

Realistic and sound approaches to the solution of the continuing problems in private school education would certainly include positive need for a side-by-side and respectful working relationship between the recognized accrediting commissions and the recognized state agencies. I think we all know there is need for improvements in the approaches being made by both groups to improve the training being conducted in private vocational schools and improve the private school image. In my opinion it would be foolhardy and almost impossible for either group to honestly claim immunity from the other.

tation of occupational outlook data for the often-harried school owner is an example of such public aid; the data would of course be supplemented with information made available to the schools on a continuing basis by industrial employers. Probably even more important than a one-sided exchange of information is the possibility of cooperative ventures. One promising project is already under way in New Jersey between the state's Education Department and a private vocational school. A counselor and an instructor from the public school system have been placed in a private school which received a contract under the Manpower Development and Training Act; they are working to improve the basic educational skills of several prospective students who wish to qualify for occupational training at the school.

In October 1968, an encouraging new attempt was made on a national basis to delineate the responsibilities of accrediting groups and to improve the cooperation between these groups. The plan calls for the National Commission on Accrediting to serve as the top coordinating body for proposed councils on Regional (higher education) and Professional (medicine and law) Accreditation, and Technical and Vocational Accreditation (including mainly NATTS, ACBS, Home Study Council and public vocational schools). The Commission will also serve as a clearing house for materials designed to strengthen the accrediting process and improve the quality of the programs and instruction among members of all associated institutions.

Job Placement

Accrediting bodies rather infrequently take account of a school's placement of graduates; but they at least do so when they visit a school applying for accreditation and at the five-year re-evaluation intervals. This would seem to be a most relevant accrediting criterion in view of the job-orientation of the schooling.

As shown in Table 4–1, most schools have a placement service for their students. Practically all schools indicated they try to place graduates of their schools; and at least three-fourths of the schools make the service available both during the student's enrollment and

TABLE 4–1

AVAILABILITY OF JOB PLACEMENT SERVICE IN 128 NATTS SCHOOLS

Period of Placement	*Percent of Schools*
While attending school	75%
Upon graduation	99
For life[a]	80

[a] A few schools indicated they place each student a maximum of three times.

while he is working at an occupation allied to the training he received at the school.

Some indirect evidence seems to demonstrate that students are pleased with the training received in private vocational schools. For example, in Chapter 9 students who attended private vocational schools reported that if questioned by prospective students, they would rate their schools highly. Furthermore, many school owners and administrators said that students were a major (and even prime) source of new students.

But even a high degree of satisfaction among the graduates of private vocational schools need not be principally the result of adequate job placement. Hence, the placement ratio for all reporting NATTS schools in 1966 was estimated at 55 percent; a higher figure might have been expected in view of the fact that nearly every school had a placement service for graduates.[13] Even the placement ratio given by 128 NATTS schools may not be conclusive, because some of the schools may have counted the number of job *referrals,* not placements. Less than 20 percent of the trade school students considered in Chapter 9 claimed they had heard of the job they ". . . obtained after leaving the school from someone working for the school"; however, that number of students was only 3 percent of the total number of NATTS students completing their courses in 1966.

Although some doubts may linger about the importance of job placement in proprietary vocational schools, there are other ways of evaluating the schools' involvement in the employment of their graduates. In the first place, several factors — including the strong motivation of private school students, the intrinsic nature of the course materials and the practical job experiences of the teachers — combine to provide an employment orientation even during the period of schooling. Secondly, many schools provide more or less formal sessions on how to prospect for a job; and the visits to schools by recruiters from industrial firms afford students an early and convenient start in jobsearching. A third consideration is the extent to which the schools follow up their students after they have secured employment, by whatever means.[14]

Student follow-up is of course an important means of determining the effectiveness of a school's training and ultimately the student's occupational progress. More than $\frac{4}{5}$ of the NATTS schools had some

[13] The placement ratio was derived by dividing the number of students actually placed in jobs in 1966 by the number of students actually completing their courses in 1966; the fraction was $\frac{19,172}{34,947}$.

[14] In a sense, this factor leads to further questioning of the significance of school figures on job placements.

student follow-up procedures although the intervals varied widely. Table 4–2 shows a sharp decline in the frequency of follow-ups in the

TABLE 4–2

FREQUENCY OF STUDENT FOLLOW-UP IN 128 NATTS SCHOOLS

Frequency of Follow-Up	Percent of Schools
Within 6 months after graduation	50%
One year after graduation	19
On an annual basis	21
Other	32

first year after graduation. Only about 21 percent of the schools followed their graduates' employment progress on an annual basis. The "other" category, about ⅓ of all schools, had some follow-up within definite time periods — including every two years, two- and five-year intervals, and one-, two-, five- and eight-year follow-ups. However, most of the replies referred to informal contacts via an alumni magazine or a semi-annual newsletter. Additional responses referred to an occasional survey of graduates; personal and mail contacts students maintain with a school; and maintenance of a roster of those graduates still seeking their first job or a change in jobs.

Licensed schools, at least in New York, must follow up their graduates three months and one year after they have left school. Beyond these periods, however, many students either change their addresses without notifying the schools or else they fail to respond to questionnaires.

Some members of NATTS favor requiring both a regular school follow-up of graduates and an examination of a student's progress records by the accrediting body. Student mailings other than questionnaires would probably insure greater response. For example, Mr. William Goddard, Executive Director of NATTS, is convinced that a school newspaper, which notes the progress of a large number of ex-students, is a most effective way of maintaining the interest of graduates. The accrediting association should also seek the impressions of employers who have hired private school graduates by following up a randomly selected group of ex-students.

In what must be a distinctive case, one school hired a certified public accounting firm to follow up the employment progress of its graduates. The Bailey Technical School of St. Louis, Missouri, received the following report:

> We have conducted a survey of the graduates of Bailey Technical School, Inc. for the period 1961 through 1965 as to the nature of their

employment and the benefits of the training they received at the afore-mentioned school.

As a result of this survey we determined that 91.42% of the replies we received were employed in a mechanical or allied occupation.

It was pointed out that this form of follow-up would probably be feasible only for certain types of school; and there could be a problem in securing enough certified accounting firms with an interest in this sort of work.

Indirect Means of Evaluating Schools

In addition to employer satisfaction, other *indirect* ways of evaluating private vocational schools are available. For example, the utilization of these schools under numerous government-financed training programs is certainly an index of the confidence placed in their courses, teachers and managements. Besides, there is the demonstrated ability of the schools to successfullly motivate and instruct many persons who failed to complete their formal schooling.

Competition between private and public vocational schools under publicly-financed programs is still another indirect way of assessing the profit-seeking schools. This would, however, be feasible only where the two types of schools offered comparable programs. But a majority of the programs taught in the proprietary schools are probably not offered in public schools or else the differences in instruction are great.[15] Collaboration between the two systems would be preferable. For instance, the basic education courses offered in the public schools could be integrated with the highly specialized occupational courses provided in the proprietary schools. In addition to concurrent education and training, increased student mobility between private and public vocational schools, community colleges and junior colleges should be expected.[16]

Since the ultimate test of both the public and private school systems is the achievements of their students, evaluation is better done directly and not by a contrived competition. Certainly, however, there will still be some cases where the private and public schools can and should be compared.

[15] As suggested in Chapter 10, the government duplication of courses effectively provided (both qualitatively and quantitatively) in the private schools would merely squander the total supply of limited resources.

[16] Students at a comparatively small number of private vocational schools (e.g., RCA Institutes) can receive some college credits if they desire to further their educations. College recognition of these schools is incidentally a form of outside evaluation.

CHAPTER 5

Diverse Instruction: For the Disadvantaged and the Gifted

"Year after year, licensed proprietary schools accept high school and even elementary school dropouts, and they provide them with skills."
— KENNETH BAILEY, A State of
New York Supervisor of
Private Vocational Schools

Administrators of private vocational schools "grade" their instructional courses and instructors primarily on their success in preparing students for direct employment. The courses are therefore job-oriented and instructors are often expected to make adjustments to varying student needs. Instructors are held accountable for the performances of all their students — probably to a greater extent than obtains in most public schools; they are expected to succeed in getting most students to complete their training.

The range of courses offered in proprietary schools reflects the diverse educational requirements for admission that are reported in Chapter 3. At times, course content and occupational objectives are relevant only to the least talented, least motivated persons. Without such courses many disadvantaged people would be completely neglected. Other courses — for example, a two-year program for electronics technicians — are nearly equivalent to the "practical" instruction of the first two years of engineering in leading universities.

The instructional programs of private vocational schools (like other educational and training resources) should be evaluated on the basis of their facility for motivating and training students of *different* abilities and interests.

Whereas this chapter and the one following contain no evaluations of teaching techniques, materials or instructors, they do demonstrate how private schools attempt to accommodate training programs to diverse students — including those who are considered "disadvantaged."

No assertions are made that all or even most private schools rank high in achieving their stated objectives. However, numerous practices and policies are worth noting; some are even "ideals" or paradigms. At times, there will only be brief mention of various teaching materials, techniques and aids. Our purpose is suggestive. However, what is mentioned is not merely nominal — it is already being applied or has proven practicable.

Private vocational schools know that most of their students are eager to see a connection between their training and the occupations they hope to enter.[1] An accommodation to this need can be achieved in many ways; and when achieved it is a prime motivation both for students who learn best in concrete situations and for students who find the postponement of rewards difficult to accept.

Concrete Training Situations

Eighty percent of the responding NATTS schools indicated that a typical full-time student spends a minimum of 41 percent of each day in a concrete instructional setting. (Many students, of course, spent more.) The private schools "simulate" shops, laboratories and even department stores; therefore the transition from school to work site is minimal. In fact, at three schools that train electronics technicians, the student enters into a "contract" (on the student application form) for a "series of planned experiments." The student signs his name to the following statement: "These experiments are especially designed so that I can, by assembling actual equipment, clearly see how electronic circuits operate."[2] In addition, the theory courses at proprietary schools are of comparatively short duration; and there are careful attempts to integrate theoretical study with the practical operations of the job site.

The training setting in automobile mechanic courses approximates a repair garage. At the Lincoln Technical Institute in Newark, New Jersey, desks that were at one time in all "classrooms" have been replaced by benches and stools. At a school in New York City automobiles are accepted from private persons and engine and body repairs are made at no charge. Newly enrolled students are immediately exposed to engines and automobiles that are kept in operating condi-

---

[1] Practical course materials, which also influence the length of a course, were among the principal reasons cited by students for attending proprietary schools in California. See Harry V. Kincaid and Edward A. Podesta, "An Exploratory Survey of Proprietary Vocational Schools," in Quirk and Sheehan (eds.), *Research in Vocational Education:* Proceedings of a Conference, June 10–11, 1966 (Madison: The University of Wisconsin, 1967), pp. 202–22.

[2] United Electronics Institute has schools in Louisville, Kentucky; Des Moines, Iowa; and Akron, Ohio.

tion. It is claimed that a student learns and "gets real satisfaction" from completing a task only by hearing sounds and seeing the movement. Naturally, the students progress from easy to more difficult tasks.

This practical type of instruction is equally important in training chefs at the Culinary Institute of America in New Haven, Connecticut. The size of the kitchens approximates those found in the outstanding restaurants the instructors once worked in as chefs; this necessitates close supervision under actual working conditions. Top-grade foods, often imported, are used so that the students will learn how such foods taste and, in addition, be able to distinguish the wide variations even within the same category of quality foods. The young men are told to taste even those foods they dislike. This is necessary because some of the students come from homes that serve beans and rice, hot bread and fried bananas. "Taste has to be cultivated, and many people actually lack sensitive taste and smell," according to Jacob Rosenthal, the school's Director.

Students in an architectural drafting course prepare complete sets of drawings for buildings. Models of the buildings are often built, on an optional basis, by talented students or, on the other hand, by those who could be motivated by such a project; as such models are in progress other students tend to become stimulated.

The Electronic Computer Programming Institute, which has franchised more than 90 schools, offers the same programming course in both its day and evening sessions. The number of instructional hours in the day course is slightly greater than in the evening course but both courses include "simulated job training." The day course is considered especially appropriate for the "green" high school graduate who is usually younger and has had less employment experience than students enrolled in the evening course.[3] At the same time, a relatively greater need for the evening school student to work full-time is recognized by extending the course over a seven-month period, whereas the day course is of three months duration.

As in other programming schools, the instructional staff at International Academy of Washington, D.C. (owned by the Lear Siegler Corporation), is convinced that their course cannot be taught with textbooks alone. Students must actually do programming and a minimum number of programs must be completed to qualify for graduation.

Massachusetts Trades Shops School (an affiliate of International Telephone and Telegraph Educational Services, Inc.) has made its

[3] An official with the Institute was convinced that the daytime course was also appropriate for training many disadvantaged persons.

mathematics courses "functional." "What is learned is immediately obvious, because a student meets it in the lab that follows the class." A demonstration lathe is installed in the classroom of the machine operator course. A student who was interviewed was convinced that the use of the same teacher for theory and shop results in a very definite and immediate connection between the two forms of instruction.

At the Electronics Training Center in Philadelphia, students are shown algebraic applications on circuits. Mock-ups and a variety of demonstrations are used. For instance, the students usually become extremely curious and interested when there is an increase in voltage for no apparent reason; such a demonstration can be effectively followed up with an explanation using physical laws.[4] Project building — e.g., hi-fi amplifiers with electronic cross-over circuits for matching speakers — has also proven to be a useful instructional device.

Use of Visual Aids and Operative Equipment

Most vocational educators recognize the importance of visual aids and operative equipment:

> Because skill development depends to a great extent on how successfully the student visualizes, understands and practices the techniques, processes and operations involved in the performance of a particular job, the field of occupational instruction is ideally suited for the use of visual materials. Films, slides, illustrations, charts, mock-ups and scale models are examples of the visual aids which vocational education teachers must know how to use effectively.[5]

Members of NATTS utilize the whole range of visual aid equipment, from colored chalk on blackboards to closed-circuit television. One school uses video-tape presentations both to orient new students and as preliminary training in drafting and mathematics.[6]

Even rather simple devices have proven extremely useful. Thus a school of drafting adapts to students who have difficulty with written instructions by having the students make clay models. As one instructor said, "This helps when a student is also unable to follow a line to its logical end." That is, problems are made concrete so that such students will ultimately be much more likely to develop the ca-

---

[4] A course in auto mechanics includes the physics of combustion and electrical hydraulics only as they relate to automobiles.

[5] John Patrick Walsh and William Selden, "Vocational Education in the Secondary School," in *Vocational Education*, 64th Yearbook of the National Society for the Study of Education, Part I (Chicago: University Chicago Press, 1965), p. 131.

[6] *NATTS NEWS*, No. 67–12, December 15, 1967.

pacity for conceptualization. At the Culinary Institute of America instructors demonstrating the many stages in a process or technique are observed in mirrors tilted above the instructors and their work tables.

Training at Various Levels
Within an Occupational Group

Two educators have described an ideal component of vocational training programs in this way:

> There is a place in the vocational-business school program to provide for the varied needs of all pupils — the above average, the average and the marginal. For example, an above-average pupil might prepare to become a stenographer; an average pupil might prepare to become a bookkeeper; and a marginal pupil might prepare to become a file clerk.[7]

This is exactly the form of flexibility that characterizes the instructional programs of a predominant number of proprietary trade and technical schools. Individual schools sometimes offer programs for automobile mechanic and body fender repair worker, machinist and machine operator, or other related combinations. Even within any one of these occupations students can naturally differ in their capabilities. The more competent students become more expert as a result of the greater number of say, engine tune-ups they perform, while the "slow students may not even be aware that they *are* slow."

Without unduly hindering the progress of the better students in the classroom, instructors try to simplify, illustrate and "probe" — and, if necessary, they slow down until students are able to proceed with ease on the "building blocks" that have been established. An instructor in a business school is able to identify his weak students after the first written test; and he asks these students to do the questions that appear at the end of each assigned chapter as an additional drill.

The Electronics Training Center (ETC) in Philadelphia has two electronics courses that offer similar training for the first few months. One course, which prepares students for servicing of home appliances (radio, television and record players), requires no background in algebra, and only two years of high school; it is primarily a "shop" course. The students receive instruction in mathematics and "theory" but not at the same level as the materials presented in the more advanced course; and more time is allocated to shop than to classroom. The other course (electronics technology) requires a high school education and a course in algebra, and it prepares students for such occu-

---

[7] Walsh and Selden, "Vocational Education in the Secondary School," *loc. cit.*, p. 119.

pations as line or service technicians and technical writers.[8] The laboratory portions of both courses are offered in the same large room; no tensions are reported to exist between the students because they are generally aware of their own aptitudes. In addition, particular interests simply differ: some competent students do transfer from the repair program to the technician program; others, equally competent, prefer to remain in the repair course because they enjoy manipulative work.

Such schools, which offer alternative but related courses, are preferable to schools which offer only one of the courses. At ETC, therefore, it is less likely that a student will be "washed out" because of poor performance;[9] at the same time, more competent students can advance a rung on their "career ladder" while they are still in school.

Training at various skill levels within an occupational group has been adopted in a Washington, D.C. program financed by the U. S. Department of Labor. Initially students will receive instruction in "communication and social skills" (similar to that available at the Opportunities Industrialization Center, described on page 88). This will be followed by four months of institutional training and eight months' on-the-job training in the culinary occupations, auto mechanical trades or the building trades. The Mayor of Washington had reason for expressing pride in the program; but he was not entirely familiar with the private schools' operations when he said: "For the first time in America we have put together a program that matches the man and the job. . . ."[10]

Motivation

The administrators and instructors of private schools have rarely benefited from or sought the professional assistance of educators, guidance counselors or psychologists to learn more effective ways of motivating students. Nevertheless, they have recognized that a student's lack of scholastic ability may be less of a handicap than the "inability" to report consistently, and on time for class. In a way perhaps analogous to the early inventors who were usually craftsmen

---

[8] This year, for the first time, each second-year student has a research project and writes a "thesis."

[9] An evening course in radio-TV repair work at a Boston school still has its students begin by building a radio in a piece-by-piece way. (Many schools have apparently discredited this learning device. Even this school has discontinued the practice in a similar course given during the day.) Presumably students who were "long-time losers" are so thrilled with the radios they have built that they would not sell them for $50. And students are able to complete this course, rather than "flunk out" of a more demanding course.

[10] Carl Bernstein, " 'Model' D.C. Job Project Set," *The Washington Post*, March 30, 1968.

and not engineers the more astute school officials have devised diverse means of stimulating their students. This is noteworthy because ". . . where motivation to succeed is minimal and there are proscriptions against competitive behavior, the individual may obtain a low I.Q. score but in fact be outstanding in one or more dimensions of intelligence. This statement [by Steven Vanderberg of the University of Louisville School of Medicine], takes on added significance when problems of educating children from so-called deprived urban environments are considered."[11] It would seem likely that many private schools have succeeded in motivating some of these students and in the process stimulated latent aptitudes.

The New Student

Private schools are generally aware of the importance of encouraging student interest from the very start of training, and the students are often urged to take advantage of the chance to "better themselves." Although professional terminology is rarely used, the schools recognize that every new student must develop a favorable "self-concept." One administrative official said that each new enrollee must be convinced "that he can move out of mediocrity." The students are therefore encouraged during the first class session with an optimistic talk. They are told that earnest effort will be expected of them, but that each student will receive consistent support and extra assistance when he needs it. The head of training at another school puts incoming students at ease by indicating that thousands of young persons with varying abilities have preceded them in training. Further encouragement is offered by stating that the training will be offered "bit by bit." They are also assured that the school knows what industry expects of new workers; and the students are impressed with the significance of their training when it is announced that their attendance and absence records will be part of the performance record submitted to prospective employers. Finally, the students, who often have a realistic and pragmatic orientation, are pleased when they are placed in training settings which are job-like. In short, the school attempts both to stimulate and to relax new students who might otherwise be discouraged, particularly in view of their public school experiences.

The approach to incoming students at the non-profit Opportunities Industrialization Center (OIC) of Philadelphia (or its other locations) necessarily differs from most proprietary schools, since the Centers have no admission requirements, and a counseling staff offers personal and vocational guidance. Prospective students are generally

[11] David C. Glass, "Genetics and Social Behavior," *Items,* Social Science Research Council, Vol. 21, No. 1 (March 1967), p. 2.

motivated or at least somewhat interested when they arrive initially, because, unlike other available training programs, no stipends are paid.

A male applicant at OIC is immediately placed in an orientation course; or he may simply be allowed to talk randomly in individual consultation in order to "calm him down." The new enrollees are told about the requirements and operations in several vocational areas and they are encouraged to ask questions. Usually within one week each newcomer is placed in the "feeder" program, which has sessions in various aspects and levels of basic education, personal development and minority history. The course in minority history is intended to give students a sense of pride. Students are told they can either brood or progress steadily from the start they are given at OIC.

The Training Period

Throughout the training course in a private school, the teacher in each classroom or workshop is primarily responsible for maintaining student interest. A drafting school in New York City has even tried to motivate some first-year students by shifting them to another instructor whose "point of view or style" may prove more acceptable.

An effective teacher convinces his learners that their study is worthwhile because they are preparing for an occupation that will afford them self-respect and status; he moreover informs them of the opportunities for occupational advancement. Some instructors have outside jobs as consultants or "trouble-shooters"; and their concrete experiences on the job reinforce the belief in the value of the schooling.

During the period of instruction the "reality" of the job-like training site is enhanced by trips to industrial exhibits and conventions. Drafting students visit buildings under construction; and students are impressed when representatives of private industry tour their schools, provide information on job opportunities, or actively recruit graduates of the school.

The Prime Mover

The instructors frequently emphasize the employment opportunities open to successful graduates. This is probably the prime means of motivation for all students, not merely the "disadvantaged". Although most students are training for initial full-time employment, many of the trainees are seeking to upgrade their present vocations. For example, ex-shipping clerks or older persons who have been in allied trades (including building construction and machine shop) that are too arduous for them, have enrolled in drafting courses.

Usually, the students are told about the specific jobs for which the schools prepare them, plus the opportunities for career progression within the occupation; but they may also be informed of the possibility of teaching or even establishing a small business in, say, automobile repairing. The President of Griswold Institute in Cleveland recounted how numerous young people who attended his schools had been motivated to enter college. A student is advised along the following lines: "Jobs as medical technicians shouldn't be the end of the road for you; try to go on to college." Typically, the students who accepted the suggestion were motivated by securing good paying jobs as technicians and working alongside engineers, scientists and physicians.

Occasionally, the appeals are rather untraditional. An instructor in electronics technology has posted want ads in the classroom for both technicians and busboys; he claims it is effective to list the considerably more numerous job openings for busboys than for technicians. At times, students are told what they could afford if they had good-paying jobs; they are asked if they would like to take a "real vacation," purchase a car or even a home.

Motivation can be applied in such intimate and sensitive considerations as personal appearance and attitudes. It is often not only a lack of money that explains the sloppy appearance and behavior of some students. At the OIC, the classroom where personal development is taught contains three mirrors and it is virtually required that students dress neatly — though not necessarily in new clothes. At a truck-driving school in Atlanta, Georgia, the trainees are taught proper grooming and they are even "instructed" on how to shake hands. Practical and perceptive school administrators have evidently recognized that employers rate "appearance" as an important part of "performance" or "service." Preparation for employment involves more than the required instruction or training in a specific occupation. Most employers also expect their employees to display responsible, dependable behavior. A school that trains in auto mechanics and auto body work maintains a tool room manned by a person who issues tools on loan to students. This procedure, it is argued, teaches responsibility, because it is necessary to remember to return the borrowed tools.

Most schools maintain a careful check over the absence and tardy records of their students. Punctuality is of course also an important concern to employers, and trainees must learn to be on time to their classes. A representative of a major life insurance company that undertook to train high school dropouts found that their real problem with these trainees was "lateness and absence records," and not ability.[12]

At private vocational schools, only limited instances of tardiness and

[12] New York, Manpower Advisory Council, *Proceedings, Governor's Conference on Manpower Training*, June 2, 3, 1966 (New York 1967), p. 84.

absence are allowed before the student receives a warning from school officials. When possible, practical remedies are offered. For instance, a young student who rode the subway from the Bronx to Manhattan was consistently late. The student said he tried his best to be on time. His instructor was able to offer a solution when he learned that the student had gotten into the habit of being at the subway stop at a specific time because he was unaware that the subway train *also* ran approximately 15 minutes earlier.

A student's deportment, personal appearance and sense of responsibility may account for one-third or more of his final grade. Students accept these aspects of training because they are told that personal pride must accompany a well-executed service.

School Owners Rank
Incentives

The member schools of NATTS were asked to list and rank the incentives they used for maintaining student interest. Table 5–1 summarizes the responses. The most frequently mentioned incentive to students was school visits by employers or their representatives. Other incentives commonly mentioned were also related to the ultimate student goal — employment. These included: vocational counseling, visits to plants or offices and demonstrations by outside visitors. The second most common motivational method was the breakdown of a course into small achievement units, which is discussed in the next section. The "other" category included such related factors as: the promise of future jobs, active placement office at the school, absence of academic subjects and visits from successful graduates. Student clubs was only mentioned six times; this of course reflects most

TABLE 5–1

MAJOR WAYS OF MAINTAINING STUDENT INTEREST,
AS REPORTED BY 128 NATTS SCHOOLS

Type of Incentive	Number of Schools[a]
Visits by employers or their representatives	58
Breakdown of course into small achievement units	54
Vocational counseling	37
Visits to plants or offices	34
Other	30
Demonstrations by outside visitors	25
Recreation activities	9
Public display of student projects	5

[a] Total exceeds 128 because multiple answers were given.

students' thoroughgoing involvement in occupational training and the frequent necessity for working after school hours.

Instructional Methods

The breakdown of a course into short, sequential units or topics is perhaps the most distinctive method of instruction found in private schools. Professor Kenneth Hoyt of the University of Iowa believes that school administrators "stumbled on" this important innovation, which provides "short-term motivations" and the first success in the lives of many students.[13] Innumerable examples of the following sort could be cited: a midwestern school that trains in electronics technology has a program consisting of "at least 150 assignments." The longest segment of a two-year course that trains for positions in the culinary field is only two weeks. A New York school has a mechanical drafting course which has a basic part of 38 units. The units represent three-fourths of the total 1,000-hour course and a letter grade is assigned for each unit. When students complete the basic part of the course, they continue in such specific areas as piping and process drafting or machine detail. Architectural drafting is also a 1,000-hour course but it is obviously geared for students who are highly disciplined, since the basic part of the course is only about 150 hours. In the balance of the course students design three different buildings: 1) a vacation house or cottage; 2) a large residence; 3) a commercial building.

This practice of presenting courses in segments reflects the following reasoning: student motivation and success are encouraged largely through a continuing sense of achievement in their vocational education. Dr. David P. Ausubel is authoritative in supporting this type of instruction:

> Psychologists have been emphasizing the motivation-learning and the interest-activity sequences of cause and effect for so long that they tend to overlook their reciprocal aspects. Since motivation is not an indispensable condition for short-term and limited-quantity learning, it is not necessary to postpone learning activities until appropriate interests and motivations have been developed. Frequently the best way of motivating an unmotivated pupil is to ignore his motivational state for the time being and concentrate on teaching him as effectively as possible. Much to his surprise and to his teacher's, he will learn despite his lack of motivation; and from the satisfaction of learning he will characteristically develop the motivation to learn more.

[13] In many trade and cosmetology schools sequential learning includes, in addition, frequent repetition of subject matter, according to a public supervisor of more than 50 schools in the metropolitan New York area.

Paradoxically, therefore, we may discover that the most effective method of developing intrinsic motivation to learn is to focus on the cognitive rather than on the motivational aspects of learning, and to rely on the motivation that is developed retroactively from successful educational achievement.[14]

The impressions of a student enrolled in a machinist course at a proprietary school are useful in illustrating Ausubel's findings. The student was a high school graduate with a C+ average and he admitted that he did not put enough effort into his studies. He did enjoy an elementary machine shop course; he worked in that occupation for a while following his high school graduation and then decided to further his education. The course materials at the private trade school interested him and he ranked himself in the top quarter of his class. "You're here to learn things. It's not like high school where you can get away with goofing off," he observed.

The entire instructional setting, teaching materials and methods in many private schools attract, stimulate and train persons who would otherwise be much less likely to attain their personal occupational objectives. Many of these schools do not want to be considered educational institutions — in part because it is recognized that their students often had unfortunate experiences in academic schools. This is why even the terminology of trade and technical schools is "non-academic." The word "program" may sometimes be substituted for "course," but at other schools the word "course" is used to represent what an academic school would designate as "subject." A "book" becomes a "training manual." The word "work" may be substituted for "training"; and this, of course, makes sense to students because the ultimate work site has usually been duplicated at the training schools.

Teaching Basic Skills

Despite the minimization of general educational content, the private schools do, as noted earlier, teach those aspects of mathematics and other subjects that are related to a particular vocational course. The trade and technical schools have also found that subjects are more likely to be learned in an informal, work-like environment. Finally, many of the schools are willing to accommodate their programs (already containing limited basic education) to a variety of academic deficiencies in their students. This is illustrated in the following brief accounts. The Germain School of Photography in New York, which may

[14] David P. Ausubel, "A Teaching Strategy for Culturally Deprived Pupils," Miller and Smiley (ed.), *Education in the Metropolis* (New York: The Free Press, 1967), pp. 293–294.

be the only recognized school to offer a course in the demanding field of medical photography, has also given oral examinations to students who could not read. A remedial form of mathematics is also offered at the school. One student who learned about logarithms is supposed to have exclaimed, "If only it had been fun like this in public school!"[15] Another school in New York City (Mandl School for Medical and Dental Assistants) finds it necessary to provide instruction in basic English (e.g., spelling and sentence structure) for students being trained as medical and dental assistants. A drafting instructor with more than 15 years of teaching experience has found that high school graduates may not be able to read intelligently; he therefore offers an oral explanation prior to assigning reading materials.[16] He has also discovered that it may be helpful to have students read about a particular subject in three or more different texts, since some authors' explanations are incomplete or unnecessarily complicated; and at times, the drawings and text may not even be consistent. A school of upholstering and floor covering must sometimes start from scratch by teaching students the concept of fractions so that they can use a yardstick. Similar experiences were reported by schools in Philadelphia and Boston offering a course in radio-TV servicing. The head of training at a school has found mathematics, spelling and writing skills so poor that "it's a mystery how the students could have graduated from high school." Some of the students who "passed" high school algebra were presumably baffled when their instructor mentioned fractions or decimals. A little mathematics had been introduced "without being identified," it was noted.

All of the above examples demonstrate that (1) some secondary schools are not providing adequate instruction for many of their students; and (2) private trade and technical schools are presumably willing to accept the challenge of redressing deficiencies in order to train these educationally "disadvantaged" persons for full-time jobs. It is moreover noteworthy that some training projects financed by the Federal Government are "discovering" the ingredients that have been

[15] The Georgia post-secondary schools have found it necessary to review mathematics extensively for their students and related the material to work. "One of the first things we find out is that they don't know much math. They spent a couple of years on algebra in high school, but because they knew they weren't going to college and because they didn't see any other use for it, they didn't learn it. Practically every course we have has math in it. So we have to pump a lot of math into them. But we relate math directly to practical work. Because it has real meaning, they learn it." U. S. Department of Health, Education, and Welfare, Office of Education, *New Directions in Vocational Education*, OE-80047 (Washington, 1967), p. 20.

[16] According to the instructor, "the problem is to pitch the material at the student's level and in language that he understands, especially in the lecture room."

widely utilized with good results in proprietary schools for several decades.[17] Thus in East Los Angeles, a "skill center" proved successful after the "usual classroom aura" was replaced by "unstructured school situations."[18]

Graduation Policies

Since securing employment related to training is the objective of instructional programs in proprietary schools, successful completion of the programs is a serious concern of students, instructors and school administrators. The graduation of students is often dependent upon demonstrated practical skills. Examples of partial requirements include writing more than 20 programs for programmers, and an "acceptable folio of photos" for photographers.

Frequently, student employability is a general requirement for graduation. Therefore the more responsible schools encourage unpromising or failing students to transfer to less demanding courses or even drop out of the school during the first month or less of instruction. Remaining students who fail to meet graduation requirements may, at many schools, repeat the course at no additional charge, except of course the additional time such students must expend. Hence, unlike some other schools, the reputable private vocational schools are extremely concerned with the performance of their graduates. This means there is a virtual guarantee of comparatively meaningful graduation for most students accepted by a school.[19] Besides being motivated by a concern for the students *per se*, school owners realize that graduates *can* markedly affect a school's reputation.

As tangible evidence of completing a course, a student receives a diploma or certificate (some states do not permit the designation of "diploma" by these schools) in whatever occupational program he is able to master. Some schools will not issue a certificate to graduates whose performance is only barely satisfactory. Such students, e.g., those studying to be medical assistants, are likely to be employable in a medical occupation, but they will generally not be able to qualify for comparatively independent work in a laboratory.

[17] Of course, the achievements of proprietary schools have remained unknown because they have been virtually ignored by academic educators and the U. S. Office of Education. In addition, the owners and administrators of the private schools are rarely scholars and there have therefore been only limited attempts to even describe the schools' operations and accomplishments.

[18] W. Stewart Pinkerton, Jr., "Slum Teachers," *The Wall Street Journal*, July 25, 1967.

[19] The graduation requirements in some occupations (e.g., medical technician) include service of an "internship." Prior to receipt of a diploma the student must complete about six months' employment and receive the employer's recommendation.

Most schools no longer nominally distinguish between levels of proficiency by issuing a diploma (signifying good achievement) and a certificate (signifying only fair or less achievement), according to William Goddard, the Executive Director of NATTS. Instead, distinctions are made on the basis of student transcripts and recommendations from the schools to prospective employers.

However, the private schools would again issue either a diploma or a certificate if they were given much more opportunity to train disadvantaged persons under government programs. Training the disadvantaged could necessitate distinguishing between levels of proficiency.

As an experiment, the Culinary Institute of America accepted randomly some 30 students who ranked near the bottom of their high school class. A substantial percentage of the students were average or better in their course; a few students even took honors; and only three of them dropped out. It was learned that students who were below average could often perform excellently in the practical phases of cooking and baking, but had trouble with cost control and management courses. As a result of the "experiment," a culinary diploma was awarded to students completing *all* requirements, and another certificate was given to students who completed only the practical portions of the course or else achieved "lower passing grades."[20]

At some schools a graduation ceremony marks the completion of a course. Naturally the sizes of the graduating classes vary widely at different schools. At a private nonprofit trade and technical school in Chicago the entire student body attends each monthly graduation exercise, since this presumably establishes an esprit de corps.[21] A lengthy tool and die designing course (requiring three to six years for evening students) only has a formal graduation ceremony when there are at least three to six men who have completed the course. On the other hand, certain schools which have students completing their courses *throughout* the year hold no graduation exercises.

[20] Although it is unlikely these students would become executive chefs, they could look forward to successful careers in less responsible jobs.
[21] *Midway Technical Institute Bulletin,* February 1967, p. 6.

CHAPTER 6

Roles of the Instructors

"We attempt to adjust a program to the student and not vice versa. We recognize their differing capabilities and therefore don't aim every student's sights to the same heights, because they could be broken for life. If a student can't become a machinist he may be a machine operator; if not a draftsman, perhaps a tracer."
— President of a Trade School

Although the use of operative equipment in a setting that simulates work sites is an important element in vocational training, the ability of instructors to motivate and teach students is even more crucial — especially in view of the varied demands made upon proprietary school instructors. It is moreover noteworthy that numerous practices that are already established in the profit-making institutions are merely exceptional cases or experiments in other schools. For instance, adaptability is considered the most important attribute of teachers in the laudable programs launched under the "Richmond Plan" in California. A teacher under that program must be able to say, "if a lot of students failed, I failed to present it right."[1] Most proprietary schools do indeed consider numerous student failures in one course, or in several courses over time, an indication of the instructor's failure.

Instructors in private vocational schools are urged that their students are "clients", not "charges". An important financial responsibility therefore resides with the school. As the supervisor of the Grantham School of Electronics in Washington, D.C. observed, each instructor must be critically evaluated, since former student referrals account for at least 50 percent of a school's student body. The schools can ensure creditable teaching performances, because typically their instructors are not given tenure.

[1] U. S., Department of Health, Education and Welfare, Office of Education, *New Directions in Vocational Education*, OE-80047 (Washington, 1967), p. 9.

Instructor Qualifications and Aids

The special instructor-student relationship in the private vocational school naturally influences the form and manner of instruction in these schools. As an example, the instructors at the Roberts' Technical Trade Schools in New York City and many other schools engage in "group teaching on an individual basis." Students proceed at the same pace in the theoretical part of their course, while different rates of progress are accepted in the practical or shop training. As noted before, students who are deficient in the theory phase of a course are encouraged to seek aid in frequently conducted review classes.

Shop training, on the other hand, is evidently more readily grasped and quickly applied, although there are differences in performance levels here too. It is therefore an instructor's responsibility to circulate frequently among individuals or small groups of students. An instructor with six months' experience said that he had to be familiar with the entire course he was teaching. Since students could enroll in the course at frequent intervals, they were always at different stages of progress.

Small classes and individualized instruction make many private schools an ideal environment for training both students who failed in secondary schools and persons with a variety of handicaps who are referred by the Vocational Rehabilitation agency. These students with varied capacities naturally demand instructors who are not limited to an unchanging lesson plan. At many schools, moreover, according to Joel Robinson, Director of the Manhattan School of Printing in New York, handicapped and disadvantaged persons are enrolled *every* four or five weeks. Instructors must therefore be exceptionally adept, since many of the disadvantaged persons have had to contend with waiting all of their lives. "They simply do not want to wait any more; perhaps they cannot wait."

Private school instructors may be further evaluated in ways that would prove exceptionally humbling to teachers in other school systems. Even the reputed sensitivities of competent chefs are challenged at one school where students rotate among chefs for instruction. It is simply recognized that different chefs have "certain flairs and distinctive touches."[2]

[2] Several aspects of instruction commonly found in private vocational schools have been recommended to elementary school educators by Dr. Harold T. Smith:

The organizational ingredients that promise to be most helpful are various combinations of smaller classes, team teaching, . . . a fuller use of specialists, and a greater use of the continuous growth organization in lieu of the con-

In view of the considerable demands placed upon private school teachers, what formal preparation, experience and talents are they expected to have? Many school administrators are convinced that "paper qualifications" are unimportant if an applicant for a teaching position knows his subject material and can teach. Educators feel that every teacher should have some liberal arts education, but they also agree that vocational instructors ". . . must first of all know, from experience, the skills and activities required for success in the occupation and must have been successful in it." Moreover, unlike teachers of agricultural, business, distributive and home economics occupations, there happen to be hardly any universities that offer instruction for the trade and technical teacher.[3]

Information on current techniques and processes within crafts and industries naturally alter some of the relevance of the earlier experiences of private school instructors. Instructors are therefore required to keep abreast of industrial changes and introduce them into their instructional courses.

As noted before, instructors and students often visit industrial plants and laboratories as a regular part of the training program. This practice, however, is exceptional in the public schools as demonstrated by the following account of the distinctive "Richmond Plan" in California:

> The benefits fall not only on students but also on teachers, who frequently have only vague notions of how people outside education do their work. The benefits of realism are also brought to the program by former pretech students. Says Mr. Johnson, the guidance counselor, "We learned from our boys who went on to get jobs as engineering, chemical and architectural technicians. A lot of them said they wished they had more drafting. So we stole a little time from our physics instruction. In the 12th year, instead of 3 days of physics and 2 of drafting, we now schedule 3 days of drafting and 2 of physics."[4]

Most of the 20 states that have statutory and regulatory provisions dealing with private vocational schools require instructors to have work experience (ranging from two years in Colorado to eight years in Massachusetts) in the vocational area they are teaching. Usually the work

ventional organization by grade. A greater shift to the continuous growth philosophy of teaching is certain to bring about its own style of group teaching; in fact, it could scarcely come about without doing so.

See Harold T. Smith, "Role of the Elementary Grades in Developing the Potentials of Disadvantaged Children, Kalamazoo County, Michigan" (Kalamazoo, Michigan: The W. E. Upjohn Institute for Employment Research, 1966), p. 22.

[3] J. Chester Swanson and Ernest G. Kramer, "Vocational Education Beyond High School," in *Vocational Education*, 64th Yearbook of the National Society for the Study of Education (Chicago: University of Chicago Press, 1965), p. 170.

[4] *New Directions in Vocational Education*, p. 9.

experience is an alternative to formal education, and no state requires more than a high school education. However, a survey of instructors in the member schools of NATTS disclosed that about 60 percent of the instructors actually had some college education and more than ⅓ of the total had at least four years of college education.[5] The larger independent schools plus those operated as subsidiaries of corporations pay the tuition of their instructors enrolled part-time in college courses that are related to their teaching fields.

The same study showed that 60 percent of the instructor training was acquired by the following related methods: teaching under close supervision, serving as an assistant to a teacher, or taking a course in teacher training provided by the employer during working hours.[6] This would appear to coincide with the work experience requirement in the states with regulatory provisions and "present some evidence that the administrator of the private occupational school is concerned with the quality of teaching."[7]

Since the private school owners and administrators expect good performance from their instructors in the face of many challenges, it is pertinent also to consider some of the aids and advantages in the instructional setting from the instructor's point of view. The student-teacher ratio is one such important consideration.

Table 6–1 shows the student-teacher ratio in the classroom (or lecture) and shop, laboratory or machine practice. The typical student-teacher ratio for classroom instruction is small, at least when compared with the ratios found in the introductory courses of many colleges and universities. Some 60 percent of the private schools have a ratio of 24 or less students per instructor. Naturally, the average ratio is lower in shop, laboratory or machine practice. Approximately 54 percent of the schools assign 19 or less students to an instructor at any given time; and only 16 percent of the schools assign 25 or more students to an instructor in the practical teaching situation.

Good vocational schools recognize that their instructors must also have effective and current course materials. The president or director

---

[5] Seven hundred twenty-six full- and part-time instructors were included in the 65 schools responding. See Eloise L. Johnson, *A Descriptive Survey of Teachers of Private Trade and Technical Schools Associated with the National Association of Trade and Technical Schools,* Doctor of Education dissertation submitted at the George Washington University on February 22, 1967. Reproduced in part by Griswold Institute Print Shop (Cleveland, 1967), pp. 57, 70.

[6] At one school, the director observes new instructors in the classroom. If the prospective teacher has slight defects or if he admits he has no experience, the director instructs him in teaching techniques; but if he says he can teach when he obviously cannot, "he would be too much of an effort to train."

[7] E. L. Johnson, *op. cit.,* pp. 80, 81, 92.

TABLE 6–1

STUDENT-TEACHER RATIOS IN CLASSROOM OR PRACTICAL SITUATION FOR RESPONDING NATTS SCHOOLS[a]

Student-Teacher Ratio in Classroom or Lecture						Student-Teacher Ratio in Shop, Laboratory or Machine Practice					
10	10–14	15–19	20–24	25–29	30+	10	10–14	15–19	20–24	25–29	30+
Number of Schools						*Number of Schools*					
3	10	26	38	27	24	8	17	41	37	16	4

[a] 128 schools provided a classroom ratio; 5 schools omitted an answer for the practical situation in their school.

of a school will usually make required revisions in consultation with his faculty, while some of the large schools, at least, point with pride to the insulation or freedom of operations that is established policy for their "business" and "education" divisions.

In general, published instructional materials are either unavailable or unusable directly for teaching purposes. Dr. Johnson found that commercial textbook publishers were a source of curriculum development in only 16 percent of the cases reported by instructors.[8]

Although their number is probably limited, there are schools which have formal divisions composed of "instructional specialists." For example, at the Opportunities Industrialization Center in Philadelphia, the "specialists" are familiar with all written course materials in their fields; and they communicate often with instructors and members of advisory committees to determine whether they must prepare original course materials. Their fields of specialization are: communication, grooming and minority history; technical courses; and computations and machine tool.

Many other schools have also prepared, printed and copyrighted textbooks and syllabi for instructors. For example, a manufacturer of computers has published operating manuals which are reputedly well prepared but presuppose some technical knowledge and therefore serve mainly as a review rather than an ideal textbook. This has influenced several computer schools to write textbooks for various computing machines and specific "languages"; and materials are continually revised to keep up with changing machinery and instructional needs.

Attempts are made at the better private schools to keep instructors abreast of changes and developments in their fields. Indeed, this is a necessity for most instructors, since courses are revised often and

[8] E. L. Johnson, *op. cit.*, p. 83.

new courses are introduced to accord with frequently swift alterations in occupational requirements. It was found that more than one-third of all courses at 128 NATTS schools had been taught for only five years or less; and more than four-fifths of all courses had been taught for 20 years or less. There are several ways of helping the instructors accommodate to such changes. For instance, schools subscribe to trade and technical journals and may encourage instructors to attend meetings of professional or technical associations. Discussions or meetings are held at some schools. Guest lecturers may be compensated, although usually a manufacturer of, say, test instruments or brake linings will provide a free demonstration to faculty and even students.

A faculty director, dean of education or "lead instructor", is responsible both for school curricula and the performance of his instructors. The supervision of instructors is surely greater than it is in most liberal arts colleges or large universities. (One school reported that it evaluates its instructors every *three* months.) In fact, there may be "tight controls" on how materials are presented and the progress an instructor has made in each course at any given time.

Teachers are expected to place special emphasis upon those parts of a course in which students have consistently encountered difficulties. In connection with this, one lead instructor suggested the possibility that certain of his colleagues may lose the "common touch" after taking several college courses; such instructors are reminded that they should be teaching at the vocational and not the college level. Attention is also given to instructors who have taught the same course several times, since they may tend to neglect basic points which are crucial to complete understanding.

The grading of students reflects both familiarity between instructor and student and a concern for minimizing the anxieties that might have resulted in the more formal situations students encountered in primary and secondary schools. Although most schools inform students of their progress by issuing letter or numerical grades only 54 percent of the schools ranked them the most important criterion. Nearly 40 percent of the schools indicated that a "review of a student's work in the classroom and/or shop" or "individual instructor-student conferences" were the principal ways of grading students.

Student Appraisal of Instructors

Many schools associated with NATTS provided letters of testimony from former students addressed to individual instructors or the school's director. This personal testimony from former students reinforces the school owners' frequent assertion that their instructors are dedicated

and earn the students' respect because of their practical experience
and teaching abilities.[9]

A survey of several hundred graduates of trade and technical schools
suggests that the responding students are very satisfied with their instructors.[10] Two of the groups studied were high school dropouts
enrolled in courses for automobile mechanics, automobile body fender
repairmen and machinists, and students being trained as technicians.
Sixty-three percent of both the high school dropouts and technicians
indicated that their teachers in private vocational schools had definitely
been "better than average," or "some of the best teachers [they] ever
had." More than 95 percent of the students in both broad groups are
accounted for, if we include the students who indicated that their
instructors were about the same as other instructors they had known.

Counseling

Student counseling is a necessary function in private schools, because it is often directly related to instruction and other student services. Moreover, instruction may be incomplete in the absence of
counseling, even though the counseling is typically given by a school's
regular instructors who are *not* licensed to offer guidance.

Deficiencies in many public school programs are a major reason
why counseling must be offered in the private schools. Inadequate
attention to the post-schooling needs of many young persons has probably been inevitable in view of the limited number of high school
guidance personnel and their equally limited "philosophy." This
means that many persons who drop out of school and even many who
graduate have insufficient knowledge of the labor market or occupational training opportunities.

Whereas the "optimum" (but certainly not the "ideal") counselor-
student ratio is authoritatively set at one counselor for every 300
students, the actual national public school average in 1963 was one
counselor for every 537 students. Dr. Henry Borow, Professor of
Psychological Studies at the University of Minnesota, found that only
a small minority of all school systems has achieved the "optimum"
ratio and many schools do not even have a single counselor.[11] Several
of Borow's findings were supported in a more recent study performed

[9] An instructor at a school in Philadelphia, who had 20 years' teaching experience in electronics and basic electricity, said that the most popular instructors
are those who set high standards for the students.

[10] From unpublished data of the Specialty Oriented Student Research program
conducted by Professor Kenneth Hoyt of the University of Iowa.

[11] U. S., House of Representatives, General Subcommittee on Education of the
Committee on Education and Labor, *Hearings on Vocational Education Amendments of 1966*, 89th Cong., 2nd. Sess., Part 1, June 1966, pp. 185, 188.

by Professor Jacob Kaufman and associates in nine selected communities in New Jersey, Pennsylvania, Maryland and Ohio. Between two-thirds and three-fourths of the 5,300 graduates of public schools claimed that "they had never discussed their job plans with a guidance counselor."[12] Such deficiencies are compounded by the fact that a large majority of school counselors have little knowledge of the "characteristics, educational motivations and educational-vocational experiences" of the students enrolled in thousands of private vocational schools.[13]

The Vocational Education Act of 1963 did concentrate on preparing students for work and this has influenced school counselors to become more attentive to vocational counseling.[14] The American Personnel and Guidance Association (APGA) was also moved to establish commissions to advance cooperation between guidance counselors and industry, and between schools and counselors at offices of the U. S. Employment Service.[15] Heroic individual efforts have also had some impact. For example, Professor Kenneth Hoyt of the University of Iowa lectured school counselors in 47 states during his one-year term as President of the APGA.

The more active will to provide vocational guidance must, of course, be supported by a sizable growth in the number of persons trained as counselors, and still additional changes in teachers' and counselors' attitudes toward vocational education. Many guidance counselors are undoubtedly still influenced by the fact that, "Throughout history the so-called intellectual occupations have been respected, but the manual trades have been looked down upon."[16] This means that teachers and counselors have actually *misguided* numerous young persons by allowing them to settle into the academic high school course — often because the only alternatives were vocational or technical schools with enrollments already at capacity or "special schools for dull pupils." A high proportion of these students graduate from high school but do not attend four-year colleges; their options include seeking employment or entrance into a community college, post-secondary vocational school or private vocational school.

Generally, the chances have been scant for students to learn about available training opportunities in the proprietary schools through the

---

[12] *Ibid.*, p. 229.
[13] Kenneth B. Hoyt, "High School Guidance and the Specialty Oriented Student Research Program," *Vocational Guidance Quarterly*, Summer 1965, p. 231.
[14] *Hearings, Vocational Education Amendments of 1966*, Part 1, pp. 37, 185.
[15] *Ibid.*, Part 2, p. 681.
[16] Franklin J. Keller, "Vocational and Educational Guidance," in *Vocational Education*, 64th Yearbook of the National Society for the Study of Education, *op. cit.*, p. 142.

auspices of public school counselors.[17] Some schools do invite the private schools to send their representatives to Career Day programs. There are also counselors who utilize the booklets on the impressions of students attending the 50 or so private vocational schools that are surveyed under Professor Kenneth Hoyt's Specialty Oriented Student (SOS) Research Program.[18] On the other hand, however, some counselors are unaware of the courses available at private schools, or else they have the firm impression that the schools are uniformly bad; catalogs and other materials sent in by the schools are not even displayed for students.

It becomes apparent that a substantial proportion of students are not familiar with the courses provided by proprietary schools, or else they learn about the schools through friends attending them, members of their families, newspaper advertisements or sales representatives of the schools. As a major consequence of these informal lines, many young persons who enroll in the schools are likely to do so with incomplete information on the nature of training, requirements of the occupation they are training for and the opportunities for advancement.

Types of Counseling

Two types of counseling services — at RCA Institutes of New York City and OIC of Philadelphia — can usefully be examined. RCA Institutes, a profit-seeking school, offers two main courses. The course in electronics technology requires the completion of high school, while a course in electronic circuits and systems is available to persons who have completed only 10 years of schooling. About one-third of the students at OIC, a non-profit school, are recipients of public assistance. The OIC offers a greater variety of courses, usually of shorter duration than those at RCA, and no formal education is required for admission. Both schools have a preparatory educational program, which varies according to individual student needs; personal counseling is available at both schools and is required for practically all students at OIC.

At RCA Institutes, more than 90 percent of even the high school graduates are unable to pass the school's aptitude test, although the students, for the most part, had studied the subjects in high school.

---

[17] In fact, the counseling has been inadequate even with respect to public post-secondary education. "A sizable but undetermined number of high school graduates could succeed in present occupational and liberal arts curriculums in the technical and community colleges, if they were helped to develop realistic goals and counseled into appropriate programs of preparation." See Dorothy M. Knoell, *Toward Educational Opportunity for All* (Albany: State University of New York, 1966), p. 20.

[18] A survey disclosed that the SOS bulletins were widely used by counselors. The counselors' major write-in suggestion was the need for surveying more schools.

Continuous counseling and, if necessary, tutoring, are available to such incoming students in a so-called "prep" program. The prep program was started in 1950 and consisted only of one term (one-fourth of a year). In 1956, two terms were made available, and by 1959 up to three terms were open to the least-prepared students. Does this indicate that public schools are not preparing their students as well as they did a generation ago? Perhaps it does. It could also mean that RCA Institutes' program is more difficult than most. However, with proper preparation, many more students can apparently be helped to qualify for a technical curriculum.

The "feeder" program at the OIC involves more extensive counseling because of the diverse educational backgrounds of the students, their personal and economic disabilities, and their inadequate knowledge of occupational requirements and labor market opportunities. Aptitude testing (over which there had originally been qualms) is now an established procedure; but unlike most other schools, the tests "screen-in" and do not "screen-out". After an early evaluation of new students' capabilities, counselors urge realism in job goals. They then indicate the range of occupations an applicant may try to prepare for.

The "feeder" students are counseled in individual booths which are surrounded by classrooms that offer instruction in communications (basic English), mathematics, minority history, personal grooming and other subjects. These subjects are preparatory to the vocational training courses, but an important subsidiary objective is the confidence and self-respect they instill in the students; it is possibly the first personal achievement for many of them.

Classes are graded; that is, they are separated by grade level and vocational interest. Teacher aides assist the instructors and the counselors also have the responsibility of visiting the classrooms and observing the progress of the students they are counseling. (This is a "team" practice and every staff member is cautioned against getting too close to students, since this could hinder their movement in progressive stages.) The slow students receive remedial assistance, while the more advanced students qualify sooner for regular occupational training; the different rates of progress are accepted — there are no feelings of insecurity in view of the non-competitiveness that supposedly prevails at the OIC.

Counseling of various sorts continues to be an important supportive service to the OIC students during their enrollment period. Student self-assurance is further bolstered by avoiding the "pure" educational courses that produced frustrations when taken in the secondary schools. Basic English, mathematics, and other courses started in the feeder program are taught, but care is taken to relate the material to the various vocational training areas. Since free tuition is the only form of financial assistance for most OIC students, other forms of guidance and aid — including advice on how to secure child day-care, loans or part-time jobs — are needed by many of the students. The students who hope to pass Civil Service examinations are carefully coached — including how to organize their time effectively and how to cope with competitive examinations.

David Ausubel has vividly described the successful results of counseling:

> By identifying with a mature, stable, striving and successful male adult figure, culturally deprived boys can be encouraged to internalize long-term and realistic aspirations, as well as to develop the mature personality traits necessary for their implementation. Hence, as a result of achieving current ego enhancement in the school setting, obtaining positive encouragement and practical guidance in the counseling relationship, and experiencing less rejection and discrimination at the hands of school personnel, higher vocational aspirations appear to lie more realistically within their grasp.[19]

At RCA Institutes, a full-time inter-term counselor is available.[20] Certain instructors devote several hours exclusively to personal guidance and tutoring. However, a major share of counseling is still the duty of every instructor.

The counseling at RCA Institutes — and even at schools with lower educational requirements for admission — should be further differentiated from the counseling at the OIC. The average age of the students, as in most proprietary schools, is lower, and therefore a smaller proportion have family responsibilities. According to one school administrator, each instructor keeps a sharp eye on his students and provides extra assistance, "up to a point," to the weak students. The school does not spend too much time with the unmotivated students, simply because it does not have adequate time and resources. The same administrator moreover observed that the students who attended his school ". . . are generally motivated and this is one big distinction between these schools and the public schools." This suggests that most of the students at proprietary schools are not among the highly demoralized students in the secondary schools, or else they have found job-oriented training *per se* a motivating experience. Nevertheless, even motivated students benefit from their instructor's counseling. For

[19] David P. Ausubel, "A Teaching Strategy for Culturally Deprived Pupils," in Miller and Smiley, *Education in the Metropolis* (New York: The Free Press, 1967), p. 295.
[20] A full-time counselor plus instructional tutoring is available for the exceptionally large number of foreign students at the school.

instance, at Southeastern University, a business school in Washington, D.C., all classes are conducted in the evenings, and most of the instructors, as well as the students, have full-time day jobs. Some of the instructors indicated that they will accept telephone calls in their offices on counseling matters and classwork assignments. The instructors may also use their business contacts to assist graduating students in finding jobs. At a New York school that provides training in seven different trade occupations, the students are briefed not only on securing a job, but also on holding the job; students are told, for example, not to boast about some of the newer techniques they have learned.[21]

This description of counseling in the typically good proprietary school should not leave the impression that such schools have ignored persons with some of the disadvantages of those enrolled at the OIC. For several decades, private schools, under the Vocational Rehabilitation Act (VRA), have been a prime source for training persons who often have severe physical or emotional handicaps. The VRA does provide for counselors, within the agency administering the Act, who work closely with the executives and instructors at the proprietary schools.

Private schools have also accepted challenges under the Manpower Development and Training Act; usually, moreover, the training has been through individual referrals rather than on a group or class basis. Midway Technical Institute in Chicago has trained a large number of persons under the Act; the school's President, L. T. Allison, has found that many of the trainees' "hostilities must be sorted out on a one-to-one counseling basis. The counseling program is the nucleus, the backbone of this program."[22]

Some of the newer schools — and perhaps certain of the established ones — have learned that it is not enough merely to motivate and train disadvantaged persons. One school trained and graduated a high proportion of "underprivileged" persons under an MDTA contract. However, not all of these graduates were to able to secure or hold jobs. This was ascribed to certain "personality" deficiencies — including such simple matters as proper grooming or how to apply for a job — that could have been corrected if counseling were available.

Although instructors can often successfully perform counseling duties, there are problems which undoubtedly require the services of professional guidance personnel. This, plus the fact that a shortage of counselors prevails, has influenced William Goddard, Executive Director

---

[21] Instructors provide job counseling at the Culinary Institute of America in New Haven, Connecticut, and several Yale Divinity students eat together with the chef-trainees and offer informal counseling.

[22] *Chicago Sun-Times*, November 21, 1966.

of NATTS, to suggest that it would make sense to subcontract for counseling services if the schools were given the public funds to pay for the counseling.[23]

A final form of "counseling" that is, and will surely continue to be provided by most private schools, is extra instructional assistance. It was noted in the discussion of the feeder program at OIC that achievement in arithmetic and basic English are crucial to a feeling of self-esteem and ultimate success in training. A similar relationship obtains for the RCA students who must try to erase their academic deficiencies (despite previous "education") and then successfully apply the basic education of the "prep" program to their training course. Most of the extra instructional aid at RCA Institutes for both the prep and regular students is provided individually or in small groups. For the year 1966–67, the ratio was five students per instructor hour of extra assistance;[24] and an average of 30 hours weekly was provided by the instructors throughout the year. Although such student aid (or makeup classes, as they are called at another school) is elective, an attendance record is kept and filed with the student record that is ultimately submitted to prospective employers.

[23] For a discussion of some novel resources for expanding counseling services, see Herbert E. Striner, "Counseling: A New Process in a Dynamic Economy," in *Preparing Counselors for Vocational Guidance*, Proceedings of the National Seminar on Vocational Guidance, August 20–25, 1967 (Conference jointly sponsored by the American Vocational Association and the American Personnel and Guidance Association), Leeman C. Joslin, Proceedings Ed.

[24] Only 6 percent of extra aid was in lecture form.

CHAPTER 7

Variety of Educational and Socio-Economic Characteristics of Students

"The Specialty Oriented Student is one whose motivations toward educational achievement are built largely around a desire to acquire a specific occupational skill or set of skills. Courses designed to broaden his potential for avocational living have little or no appeal to this student. He may be described as expressing relatively more interest in being 'trained' than in being educated."

— PROFESSOR KENNETH B. HOYT[1]

This chapter is largely based upon responses to the section of the long questionnaire dealing with selected educational and socio-economic characteristics of students in 128 member schools of NATTS.[2] Special emphasis is placed upon the differences between educational requirements and students' actual qualifications. The students' principal means of financing their educations are described. Reasons for student dropouts are presented, including financial problems, lack of ability for or lack of interest in a course and personal or family problems. In the succeeding two chapters, a closer examination is made of the relationship of students' financial resources and formal education with their work and study habits and performance in private vocational schools.

Differences between Educational Requirements and Students' Actual Qualifications

In general, there was a striking difference between the formal educational requirements for admission to a trade or technical school and the students' *actual* qualifications. Whereas Chapter 3 indicated that 45 percent of the NATTS schools (accounting for 37 percent

[1] From *An Introduction to the Specialty Oriented Student Research Program at the State University of Iowa* (Iowa City, 1962).

[2] See Appendix II for a copy of the questionnaire.

of all courses) require less than a high school diploma or its equivalent, 95 percent of the schools reported some high school graduates in their day classes; 81 percent reported high school graduates among their evening students. The median percentages of day and evening students with a high school education were 90 and 80 percent, respectively. In addition, although only 5 schools had one or more courses that required more than 12 years of formal schooling, 70 percent of the schools had some day students with that much schooling, and more than 50 percent of all schools had such students enrolled in evening classes.

The figures in Table 7–1 demonstrate that many students in ⅔ of the responding schools were "over-educated" — i.e., their actual education exceeded the schools' requirements.[3] Admission requirements were relaxed in about 10 percent of the reporting schools so that some of the students accepted had qualifications that were lower than the stated requirements. School requirements and actual student qualifications were approximately equal in only 16 percent of the schools; and a

TABLE 7–1

COMPARISON OF EDUCATIONAL REQUIREMENTS FOR ADMISSION
AND STUDENTS' ACTUAL QUALIFICATIONS
AT 112 RESPONDING NATTS SCHOOLS[a]

Comparison of Educational Requirements and Students' Qualifications	*No. of Schools*	*Percent of Schools*
1. Under-educated (requirements exceed actual education)	11	9.8%
2. Requirements equal actual education	18	16.1
3. Over-educated (actual education exceeds requirements)	74	66.1
4. Flexible (school includes both over- and under-educated)	9	8.0
	112	100.0%

a The data necessary for making comparisons were available in only 112 out of 128 schools filling out the questionnaire.

"flexible" admission policy that included both the over- and under-educated obtained at another 8 percent of the schools.

Any criticism of the 20 schools (categories 1 and 4 in Table 7–1) that admitted students with less than the stated educational requirement must be tempered for several reasons.[4] In the first place, some

---

3 Educational requirements were considered equal to students' actual education when the difference was only one student in either direction.

4 Critics could accuse the schools of lowering their standards simply to maximize their enrollments.

of the schools may have set (or raised) their requirements partly to accord with generally rising education levels in the population, rather than the amount of education necessary for job training.[5] Secondly, as noted previously, admission to more than 50 percent of the courses in all reporting schools did require adequate performance on an achievement or aptitude test; and the school's experiences have proved that the tests (which are often highly practical) are more accurate indicators of how a student will fare in his courses than the number of formal schooling years he has completed. (Chapter 9 does demonstrate that the performance of high school dropouts in trade schools and in the labor market is not substantially different from that of high school graduates.) Thirdly, as explained before, many schools offer a variety of courses, so that it is possible for a student who does not make the grade in one course to transfer to another. Finally, the number of students involved in the dilution of admission standards averaged only 45 students per school, or less than 10 percent of the number of students attending a typical school annually.

The really exceptional finding concerned the high percentage of schools with students whose actual education exceeded admission requirements. This is, of course, partly a reflection of a period of rising school attainment. Some of the "over-educated" students could have been methodically supplementing their formal education with the more practical instruction available in the proprietary vocational schools; and comparatively new fields like computer programming might not have been available in high school or even in some colleges. Undoubtedly, however, some of the students were simply miscounseled (or not counseled at all) into seeking more education than was essential to their needs and preferences. School owners did indeed report that college dropouts were enrolling in their programs. Although the highest requirement in 107 out of the 112 schools was only a high school diploma, 2,021 day and 768 evening students had more than 12 years of education.

An unknown but certainly large amount of additional schooling is the result of well-intended social and parental pressures. In the process many students are diverted from instructional programs they prefer, and a substantial number of them also fail to receive adequate vocational preparation.

From another viewpoint, the schools with "over-educated" students are a potentially good resource for training persons with somewhat lower educational qualifications than those actually held by the en-

---

[5] The director of one school that enrolls several hundred students stated that only the top one-third of the high school applicants were being considered for admission.

rolled students. For instance, at least 8,500 additional students with less schooling than those already enrolled could have been accommodated in only the 74 schools shown in Table 7–1.[6]

If these experiences could be generalized, it would mean that many private trade and technical schools have the capacity to train persons who would otherwise be excluded from schools with higher formal education standards.[7] Opportunities for specific training could be made available at various periods of personal occupational development, including: initial entrance to the labor market, upgrading within an occupation and training of the unemployed for a new occupation.

Enrollment by Sex and Age

Enrollees in the NATTS schools are predominantly men, although several schools do provide considerable training opportunities for women. Fifty percent of the schools had all male enrollments in their daytime classes; and more than ⅖ of the schools had only men in their evening sessions. Nearly ⅔ of the schools had at least 90 percent male enrollments in both day and evening sessions. On the other hand, less than 10 percent of the schools had day enrollments of 90 percent or more women.

Data on the ages of students attending trade and technical schools provide an indirect, but fairly clear picture of the students' employment status. The median age of students enrolled in day sessions was approximately 20, and only slightly more than 10 percent of all students were at least 26 years old. It is therefore unlikely that a sizable percentage of all these students had full-time employment experience; and Chapter 8 shows that most of the students who were employed worked on a part-time basis. In sharp contrast, nearly ⅖ of the evening students were 26 years and over. It is likely that most of these students once had full-time jobs and a high percentage of them undoubtedly still found it necessary to work full-time during the day.

An additional question to the NATTS schools concerned the age range of students during the years 1965–67. The median age for the youngest students at that time was 17, and the median age for the oldest was a rather surprising 48. Many state school attendance laws regulate the minimum age for enrolling in private vocational schools;

[6] This was estimated in the following way: 1,401 students could have enrolled in courses requiring no education to six years of education; since only 24 such students were registered, the potential net was 1,377 students. For persons with 7–9 years of schooling the potential net was 4,581 students; and for persons with 10–11 years of school the number of students was +2,507.

[7] It was indicated in an earlier chapter that the typical school operated at about only 60 percent of its capacity.

a substantial number of young persons are currently enrolled, and the average enrollment age would probably be still lower if permitted by state legislation. As regards older students, some schools even had students who were in their 60's. Athough older students were a very small percentage of total enrollment, they represented still another example of the schools' adaptability.

Distance of Students' Homes from School

In general, most students did not have to travel great distances to school. Nevertheless, at least ⅓ of the schools had a majority of students whose homes were more than 50 miles from school; and a smaller, but still substantial number of schools enrolled a majority of students whose permanent homes were in a different state. Many of these students set up temporary residence in the vicinity of the school; such an adjustment is usually some indication of a student's motivation and personal independence.[8]

More than ⅔ of the schools had some foreign students who were in the United States only for the purpose of schooling. These students totaled 914, an average of about 10 per school. Although this enrollment is a credit to the reputed standards of the schools, it is no match for the foreign student enrollment at RCA Institutes in New York City — nearly 700 students from 75 countries in the fall of 1967.

Student Finance

Only a small minority of students attending trade and technical schools can rely upon their parents or their personal savings for all of the funds to pay for their schooling. This generalization is based upon: the results reported in the following chapter; the more extensive findings generated by the ongoing Specialty Oriented Student Research Program at the University of Iowa; and 128 responses from members of NATTS to a question on loans.

Approximately ⅖ of the responding members of NATTS indicated that some of their students received loans either from banks or directly from school funds in 1966. The bank loans were extended primarily under the National Vocational Student Loan Insurance Act of 1965 (NVSLIA).[9] The school owners estimated that only 10 percent of all their students acquired the major part of their financing through loans.

Before passage of the NVSLIA, many schools assisted an unknown

[8] The schools usually help students find housing. A small number of schools even offer dormitory facilities.

[9] Mr. William Goddard estimated that by August 1968, ¾ of all members of the association had been approved for participation in the NVSLIA.

(but comparatively small) number of students in several unorganized ways. Certain schools guaranteed bank loans and they were compensated only after the loans had been repaid. Many schools have also made informal financial concessions to students (or their families) if they were impressed with their determination and dependability. For instance, at a school in Jacksonville, Florida, some indigent students were allowed to pay as little as $5–$10 weekly, or even monthly, and complete payment after they secured full-time work. A few maintenance and office jobs at the school itself were reserved for needy students. At times, some students were urged to stop their schooling for a few months and work full-time; this was in part a test of the students' "sincerity." Generally, however, it was found that "a sort of self-selection" occurred: Only the most motivated and dependable students would venture to make such special financing arrangements.[10]

A deferred payment system has been the most important form of direct financial assistance to students by the private vocational schools. More than 60 percent of 126 responding NATTS schools indicated they used the system, which is, of course, a form of short-term credit.[11] There was a tendency for the schools with loan programs to also have deferred payment arrangements (positive correlation of .67).

Scholarships and free tuition schools are not common among private vocational schools, but their existence is still noteworthy. An undetermined number of schools have provided a few scholarships to deserving students each year. It is conceivable (but by no means proven) that the private nonprofit schools are more likely to offer scholarships on an individual basis than the private proprietary schools. The Institute of Design and Construction, a nonprofit school which trains draftsmen and technicians for the building industry, has set up a $120,000 fund to provide 10 scholarships annually over a 10-year period; the grants for the Brooklyn, New York school will be made to "underprivileged teenagers" who are high school graduates.[12] The Private Vocational School Association of New York (comprised mainly of profit-seeking schools) has had several different scholarship programs; and shortly after the assassination of Reverend Martin Luther King, the Association established a scholarship program for 100 students. Seventy-five members of NATTS have also contributed $150,000 to a scholarship fund that will be used to pay the tuition of disadvantaged students applying to the contributing schools.

[10] Another school owner "adjusts tuition according to need."
[11] Students who pay their tuition in advance are in fact charged less than those making deferred payments. For instance at a school in Ohio, "tuition discounts" are offered for tuition payments made one week in advance.
[12] *The New York Times,* June 25, 1968.

A complete list of the free tuition schools is unavailable, but brief accounts of four distinctive types follow.

The William Hood Dunwoody Industrial Institute of Minneapolis, Minnesota offers scholarships for the first six months of training and student loans for any part of the balance of a course.[13] According to the school's catalog, "The actual cost of providing the instruction and maintaining the training facilities greatly exceeds the fee charged for each training period."

The Williamson Free School in Media, Pennsylvania, awards 80 full resident scholarships yearly. "The grant is, in essence, an agreement between the school and the receiver. The school provides the scholarship, . . . and the student agrees to give a portion of his time and talents to fill the many needs of Williamson's co-curricular program and maintenance of its building and campus." Unlike most private trade and technical schools, this school's mechanical trades program contains English "and other necessary subjects, including the inculcation of spiritual values." The program is three years in length and has a minimum age requirement of 16.[14]

The Hannah Harrison School in Washington, D.C. is the third type of nonprofit school. It enrolls women from age 18–55 in either practical nursing or administrative housekeeping courses. "Motivation is a prime qualification," for admission, but students must also be high school graduates or the equivalent. Free room, board and tuition are provided in exchange for duties in the students' dining room and on the dormitory switchboard.[15]

A fourth type of private nonprofit vocational school — the Bramson ORT (Organization for Rehabilitation through Training) Trade School in New York City — bears some resemblance to the previously discussed OIC in Philadelphia. However, the ORT School primarily serves *newcomers* to the United States by providing tuition-free training.[16] There is no minimum educational requirement for admission to the school which was organized in 1942 to train incoming refugees.[17] Although nonsectarian, ORT is a Jewish-sponsored organization and most of its trainees have been Jewish. Plans to close the school were canceled by the influx in recent years of homeless persons from Hun-

---

[13] Nearly 60 percent of the students work part-time.

[14] As indicated before, most programs in proprietary schools are less than two years and have a minimum age requirement of 17.

[15] A description of the Hannah Harrison School appears in an article by Lydia Van Zandt in *The Christian Science Monitor*, June 14, 1968.

[16] ORT may be the world's largest nongovernmental agency providing vocational training: it has schools in more than 20 countries.

[17] When spaces were available, the school has accepted elderly people and illiterates, and enrolls handicapped Americans (including deaf mutes).

gary, Rumania, Cuba, Argentina and other countries. About 700 persons were trained as power sewers and cutters for the garment industry during 1966. The following patterns among current ORT trainees reflect the successful job adjustments and upgrading of large numbers of earlier immigrants.

> An increasing number [of ORT trainees] are second and third members of the family to attend. A father who has been placed successfully on a job will send his wife or daughter. Students who have made the grade in the industry at entry level occupations as operators, return to learn pattern making, cloth cutting or fabric grading to move up the ladder occupationally and financially.[18]

Federally Insured Loans

In the absence of massive scholarship or tuition grant programs for students enrolling in private vocational schools (both being highly unlikely), a liberalization of the federally insured loan program would be the ideal way for helping many persons seeking occupational training. The greater availability of loans under more acceptable financial terms would also remove the principal cause of student dropouts.

However, an actual expansion in the volume of loans would only occur if prospective borrowers were carefully informed about the opportunities that could be opened up through readily available credit. An administrator at a leading technical institute claims that students from low-income families must initially be convinced that most economic activity is based upon credit. It seems that borrowing (at least for purposes of an education) is done primarily by persons from middle-income families.[19] Counselors in proprietary schools often find it difficult to convince students of the wisdom of borrowing in order to decrease the number of hours they must work after school.[20] Apparently students from poor but independent families are proud and hence unlikely to apply for loans. (When necessary, some of these students prefer to get along with little food for several days, according to a school counselor.) Another inhibiting factor for some students is the relative pessimism they hold out for their futures.

The ideal period for counseling students regarding vocational prospects, including available loans, would be during the primary, inter-

[18] *ORT Bulletin*, American ORT Federation, Vol. XXII, No. 2, May 1968, p. 6.

[19] Even former President Lyndon B. Johnson urged passage of a loan program for *middle-income families* in his 1965 message on education. See the *Congressional Quarterly Weekly Report*, No. 37, Sept. 15, 1967, p. 1807.

[20] This challenge has also been encountered at the Federal City College in Washington, D.C. See Andrew Jamison, "Federal City College: Trying to be 'Relevant'," *Science*, Vol. 161, No. 3845, Sept. 6, 1968, p. 996.

mediate and secondary school years.[21] Students do learn about loan programs from guidance counselors — but typically it is the college-bound students who "knock on the door of the counselors." In view of the inordinately heavy counseling load, students who are not college-bound tend to be seen last, if at all. In addition, many young persons decide rather suddenly to attend a private vocational school. For all of these reasons, vocational students who have decided to apply for a loan often arrive at banks later than students planning to enter college — only to learn that the banks have already fully committed their educational loan funds for the period. In any case, banks probably favor young men from higher income families who are more likely to have bank accounts.

Dropouts from Private Vocational Schools

Public school dropouts have undoubtedly been an important source of student enrollments in *all* private vocational schools. This is understandable in view of the fact that 35 percent of the students enrolled in high schools fail to graduate.[22] Nevertheless, dropouts enrolled in the schools considered in this and the following two chapters have comprised less than 20 percent of the student bodies. These schools, however, are probably not typical of thousands of other trade and technical schools; and, as shown before, a much larger number of non-high school graduates could have been accommodated even at these schools.

The surveyed members of NATTS report surprisingly low dropout rates for their schools. The median dropout rates for all day and evening classes were respectively 14 percent and 20 percent; the modes for classes in the two time periods were 10 percent and 50 percent.[23]

Financial problems were the major cause for dropouts among both day and evening students (see Table 7–2). Personal or family prob-

---

[21] A report prepared for the Philadelphia Board of Education recommends introduction and "intensification [of] career preparation activities at all levels in the school system." See University City Center, *Career Development*, Philadelphia, July 1967, p. 59.

[22] Grant Venn, *Man, Education, and Work* (Washington, D.C.: American Council on Education, 1964), p. 2.

Even 65 percent of all entrants to the labor force of a state like California, which has pioneered in expanding educational opportunities, were dropouts from either high school or college. See *The New York Times*, April 21, 1968.

[23] Since students both enroll and graduate at frequent periods during the year the question on dropouts was worded as follows: "Approximately what percentage of the day and evening students who were expected to graduate from your school in 1966 did *not* actually do so?"

TABLE 7–2

**MAJOR REASONS FOR FAILURE OF DAY AND EVENING STUDENTS
TO COMPLETE COURSES IN NATTS SCHOOLS, 1966[a]**

Major Reasons for Not Completing Courses	Day Students By Percent	Evening Students By Percent
Financial problems	61.7%	53.1%
Personal or family problems	44.5	51.6
Secured full-time job	28.1	17.2
Generally low motivation	21.9	14.1
Lack of ability for the course	14.8	7.8
Drafted into military service	9.4	3.9
Lack of interest in the course	7.8	4.7
Other	7.0	18.0

[a] The schools selected the two major reasons as they applied to both day and evening students. Since all answers are recorded in this table, the totals exceed 100 percent.

lems were the next most commonly stated reason, although its importance was somewhat greater for evening students. More than 25 percent of the schools indicated that the main reason their day students dropped out was to accept a full-time job; this percentage was higher than for evening students who were more likely to have held such jobs while attending school.[24] The evening students were also less likely to quit school due to what the schools termed low motivation. Lack of ability for a course was listed by only 15 percent of the schools enrolling day students and about half that figure for schools with evening students.[25] The "other" category was especially important in several of the schools enrolling evening students; the foremost reason was conflicts between working and school.[26]

[24] The director of a private vocational school wrote that schools like his have less control over students than colleges which operate on a semester basis and give credit only for completion of an entire semester's study. In contrast, he continued, students may leave a vocational school when they feel they have learned enough to secure a job. Also, some students are so good that they "burn up" a course quickly and ". . . we could, but don't believe in, merely padding a course with extras."

[25] A representative of a non-NATTS technical school, with a dropout rate exceeding 50 percent, said that lack of ability was rarely the principal reason. Generally, it was a "matter of frame of mind or lack of self-discipline and proper work habits."

[26] Four schools mentioned the difficulty of sustaining students' interest in evening courses requiring three to five years to complete.

CHAPTER 8

Student Finances at RCA Institutes

This chapter provides some insights into the financial needs, opportunities and preferences of students enrolled in a private vocational school. The source materials are primarily responses to a questionnaire by nearly 700 students at RCA Institutes in New York City, one of the nation's oldest and largest proprietary schools offering courses only in electronics.[1]

Students were divided principally into borrowers under the National Vocational Student Loan Insurance Act of 1965 (comprising 16 percent of all students) and non-borrowers.[2] Questions dealt with relative preferences for borrowing, working, or some combination of the two while attending school.

A choice of explanations for not borrowing was offered to non-borrowers; and the borrowing students were asked to indicate whether or not they were interested in increasing outstanding loans. Some suggestive findings regarding student attitudes toward school, work and their futures also resulted from the questionnaire.

Nature of Students in Survey

A total of 687 students completed questionnaires that were usable for the purposes of this study.[3] The responding students were generally distinguishable on the basis of 1) borrowing status and 2) type of program in which they were enrolled:

Borrowing Status	Instructional Programs
110 borrowing students	273 students enrolled in Electronics Technology
577 non-borrowing students	414 students enrolled in Electronics Circuits and Systems
687	687

[1] Students in 38 classrooms or laboratories completed the questionnaire during regular class periods on February 16, 1968. A copy of the questionnaire appears in Appendix III.

[2] The test for differences between percentages is the principal statistical test utilized in this chapter. Percentages are not carried to one decimal point, as they are in other sections of the book.

[3] It was not possible to tabulate the answers to an additional 32 questionnaires.

Sixty-one percent of the students were enrolled in the Electronics Circuits and Systems (C&S) program and 39 percent in the Electronics Technology (ET) program; and the borrowers were distributed in nearly the same proportion between the two (i.e., 59 percent of the borrowers were in the C&S program). All of the students were enrolled in one of 4 terms in the first year of either program. The ET course is two years in length and C&S takes one and a half years to complete.[4]

The ET course requires high school graduation for admission; although the C&S course demands only 10 years of schooling, about 90 percent of the students enrolled in the course were high school graduates. Moreover, most of the students reacted positively to a statement concerning the value of a high school education. Eighty-seven percent of all students "agree strongly" or "agree somewhat" that "a high school education is worth all the time and effort it requires." The typical student at RCA Institutes therefore must be distinguished from "disadvantaged" persons who have had little formal schooling or else failed to see the usefulness of their education. Of course, the students at the RCA school may still have to overcome disabilities of a financial, physical or emotional nature.

Age

The mean age of all students was 22. The borrowers' average age was 21. Non-borrowing students were in a wider age range — 17–50 years compared with 18–32 years for the borrowers. Only about 5 percent of the students were older than 31; hence the tendency for relatively older persons not to borrow to finance their training.

The greater likelihood of borrowing among younger students is also apparent when the percentage of borrowers in each term is compared with the percentage of the total student body enrolled in the corresponding term. In Table 8–1, the comparison of term 4 with term 1 is especially striking. Term 4 contained 13 percent of the borrowers but 19 percent of the first-year students. The term 1 students had 40

TABLE 8–1

COMPARISON OF BORROWING STUDENTS WITH TOTAL
STUDENT ENROLLMENT, BY TERMS

Term	1	2	3	4
Borrowers	40%	24%	23%	13%
Total Enrollment	28	30	23	19

[4] Chapter 5 points out that practically all students at RCA Institutes must complete a preparatory program offered by the school.

percent of all borrowers, although they represented only 28 percent of the student body. Besides showing relatively greater borrowing among the somewhat younger students, this might also signify a current upward trend in student interest in borrowing and/or the banks' greater willingness to extend loans.

Race

The two main racial groups at the school were white and Negro, with whites accounting for 87 percent of the student body and Negroes 10 percent. Data on the 60 Negroes who identified themselves suggest that these students were sharing somewhat more than was proportionate to their number in the loan program, but proportionately less in the ET instructional program. About 18 percent of the Negroes had received loans. Fourteen of the Negro students (or 23 percent of the Negroes reporting) were enrolled in the ET program which offers better job opportunities to the successful graduate than the C&S program.

Home Address

Ninety-five percent of all first-year students in the survey listed their home addresses in the states of New York and New Jersey.[5] As seen below, 81 percent of the borrowers lived in New York, whereas that state accounted for only 69 percent of all students. New Jersey's borrowers were in lesser proportion to the total number of students enrolled from the state. The differences in borrowing tendencies between these two states (which accounted for 97 percent of all borrowers at the school) could be attributed to at least two factors: 1) the extent to which high school counselors inform students of the availability of loans, and 2) the willingness of bankers to extend loans to vocational students. Another important consideration was that New York had a loan law prior to the enactment of a federal loan act. Also, a large bank with several offices in the metropolitan area had agreed in December 1967 (or about three months prior to this survey) to make loans to RCA students for virtually any amount requested.[6] Although only a few students had applied for these loans up to the time of the survey, the availability of such loans, plus the earlier enacted state loan act, would presumably mean that the New York students

[5] RCA Institutes has hundreds of foreign students in attendance. However, these students were excluded from the survey because they cannot qualify for the loans under the federal loan act.

[6] The loan is actually made to parents or guardians who must, of course, be acceptable to the bank. Repayments of a loan are made over a four-year period and therefore a student would presumably assume payments after he graduates.

TABLE 8–2

PERCENTAGES OF BORROWING STUDENTS
FROM NEW YORK AND NEW JERSEY

	New York	New Jersey
Borrowers	81%	16%
Percent of Total Enrollment	69	26

would be more knowledgeable about the principles of credit than the students residing in New Jersey.

Attitudes of "Typical" RCA Institutes Student

Several "life adjustment" statements on the questionnaire were intended to measure the relative self-confidence of the students and the optimism with which they viewed their futures. Such considerations would appear to have some relationship to borrowing propensities among the students. Although no clear-cut or decisive generalizations can be made on the basis of these attitudinal responses, it is possible to present a cautious view of the attitudes of the "typical" RCA Institutes student.

The average student (both borrower and non-borrower) appears to have firm confidence in his capabilities, according to responses to this statement: "I feel that if I try hard enough, I have a good chance of succeeding at whatever I want to do." On a scale ranging from strong agreement (#1) to strong disagreement (#5), the average answer was 1.4. Stated somewhat differently, 94 percent of all students (and 97 percent of the borrowers) "agree strongly" or "agree somewhat" with the validity of the statement. Eighty-nine percent of all students (91 percent for borrowers, 88 percent for non-borrowers) "agree strongly" or "agree somewhat" with the following statement: "I feel I am as capable and smart as most other people."

The typical student also believes in the value of schooling and hard work. He views the future hopefully but he is not unduly optimistic. Student answers also reflect strains of realism: One should not depend upon luck; and other people should not necessarily be expected to be helpful.

In general, the responses to "life adjustment" statements do not differ markedly among borrowing and non-borrowing students. When there are meaningful differences, they are noted in the discussion that follows.

Hours of Home Study

A comparison of study habits among borrowers and non-borrowers disclosed hardly any differences between the two. Both groups of students averaged about 11 hours of study per week.[7]

A distinct difference, however, was evident when students in the two instructional programs were compared (see Table 8–3). Whereas 32 percent of the ET students studied only 10 hours or less weekly, nearly twice that percentage of C&S students studied as much. In contrast, more than twice the proportion of ET students (compared with those in the C&S program) indicated they studied at least 16 hours per week. Additional data disclosed a general upward trend in study hours in terms 1–4 for students in the ET program, while the hours of study in the other program were uniform in all terms. The differences in required hours of study can be readily understood in view of the fact that subjects in the ET program are accepted as entrance requirements at such leading universities as the Massachusetts Institute of Technology, the Polytechnic Institute of Brooklyn, Yale, Columbia and New York University.

TABLE 8–3

WEEKLY HOURS OF STUDY FOR STUDENTS ENROLLED IN C&S AND ET PROGRAMS, BY PERCENTAGES

Instructional Program	*Hours of Study*				
	5 hrs or less	6–10 hrs	11–15 hrs	16–20 hrs	21–25 hrs
C&S	28%	34%	20%	12%	7%
ET	12	20	26	23	18

Student Employment

More than ⅔ of the first-year students enrolled at RCA Institutes were employed on a part- or full-time basis at the time of the survey. The students worked an average of 22 hours weekly, and about 14 percent of the students worked 36 hours or more weekly.

The students who were borrowers were more likely to work than the non-borrowers; the respective employment rates were 78 percent and 66 percent, and this difference was significant at the .001 level.[8]

[7] The question dealing with hours of study was undoubtedly misinterpreted by some of the students who indicated they studied five hours or less weekly.

[8] The level of significance for differences between percentages will often be indicated in this chapter by the expression ($p = .001$), which will signify that the difference was significant at the .001 level.

Also, the borrowing students averaged slightly more hours of work per week; 72 percent of the borrowers worked at least 20 hours weekly. Financial necessity among the borrowers was also evidenced by the pressure upon more than ¼ of them to hold jobs they apparently disliked. Twenty-eight percent of the borrowers, as opposed to 17 percent of the non-borrowers ($p = .001$) agreed strongly or agreed somewhat with the following statement: "Most work is dull and boring and I wouldn't do it if I didn't need the money." Only 34 percent of the borrowers (in contrast to 48 percent of the non-borrowers) disagreed strongly with the statement ($p = .001$).

In short, the borrowers were more likely to find it essential to hold jobs and to work somewhat more than non-borrowers. This need to supplement loans and other sources of personal income must be considered along with the finding that the borrowers study about as much as non-borrowing students.

As in the case of home study, students' employment differs in the two instructional programs. The proportion of employed students in the ET program declines from 79 percent to 59 percent between terms 1–4, while it increases in the C&S program from 69 percent to 78 percent ($p = .001$ for students in terms 2–4).[9] In all 4 terms, the ET students average a smaller number of work hours per week than the C&S students.

Main Reasons for
Student Employment

Table 8–4 shows the principal reasons why students, both borrowers *and* non-borrowers, worked while they were enrolled at the technical school. Only 10 percent of all students indicated they worked for the

TABLE 8–4

MAIN REASONS FOR STUDENTS WORKING WHILE ATTENDING RCA INSTITUTES, IN PERCENTAGES BY BORROWING STATUS

	Pay for Tuition and Books	Pay for Tuition, Books, and other Expenses	"I Enjoy the Work"	Work Related to Course	Combination of Expenses, including Rent, Food, Clothing, Family Support and Pocket Money
Borrowers	7%	59%	1%	6%	27%
Non-Borrowers	11	56	5	6	22
Total	10	56	4	6	24

[9] The maximum and minimum employment rates were reached in term 3: 83 percent of the C&S students worked compared to 47 percent of the ET students.

purpose of paying for their tuition and books. More than half the students were represented in the second column, which included "other expenses" (besides tuition and books). Hence most working students had to earn amounts that covered more than just their expenses for tuition and books. The other large category, accounting for about ¼ of all students, included expenses for a variety of family responsibilities. Only 10 percent of the job-holding students worked primarily because they enjoyed it or found it related to their courses.

Primary Source of Financial Support

As shown in Table 8–5, the primary source of financial support is sharply distinguishable on the basis of the students' borrowing status. Loans were the major source of funds for 43 percent of the borrowing

TABLE 8–5

PRIMARY SOURCES OF FINANCIAL SUPPORT FOR STUDENTS AT RCA INSTITUTES, IN PERCENTAGES BY BORROWING STATUS

	Employ-ment	Savings	Parents	Loan	G.I. Bill	State Aid	Other
Borrowers	28%	4%	14%	43%	10%	—%	1%
Non-Borrowers[a]	23	10	37	2	19	6	3
Total	24	8	33	9	18	6	2

[a] The small percentage of "non-borrowers" who listed loans as a primary source of support evidently were referring to personal loans made by family members or friends.

students, whereas parents served as the principal support for 37 percent of the non-borrowers. About ¼ of all students listed employment as their primary source of income. However, when the assistance of parents, savings, the G.I. Bill and state aid were combined, they accounted for 72 percent of the principal sources of support among non-borrowers, but *only* 28 percent for the borrowing students.

Students' Preference for Working or Borrowing

Although employment was the main source of financial support for only about 25 percent of all students, more than ⅔ of all students nevertheless did hold jobs while attending school. One question dealt specifically with the students' relative preference for borrowing or working to meet all expenses while enrolled at school, and Table 8–6 summarizes the results. Only 26 percent of even the students already borrowing indicated they would like to meet *all* expenses by borrow-

TABLE 8–6

STUDENTS' PREFERENCES FOR BORROWING OR WORKING
TO MEET ALL SCHOOL EXPENSES, IN PERCENTAGES
BY BORROWING STATUS

	Work to Meet All Expenses	*Borrow to Meet All Expenses*	*Combination of Working and Borrowing*
Borrowers	24%	26%	50%
Non-Borrowers	53	18	29
Total	47	20	33

$p = .001$ for all comparisons between borrowers and non-borrowers

ing, whereas 50 percent of these students indicated they would like to combine borrowing with working to meet their financial needs. The non-borrowers have a clear preference for working; however, 47 percent of these students (in contrast to 76 percent of the borrowers) did state they favored either borrowing or the combination of borrowing and working to meet all of their expenses.

Relative preferences for working or borrowing were also examined on the basis of student enrollment in the ET and C&S programs. In general, the C&S students had a greater preference for working. Although the ET students favored borrowing to a greater extent, the maximum number of students indicating this preference in any ET term was 30 percent. These results are consistent with the higher average hours of home study expected of the ET students.

Additional questions were raised in order to ascertain whether the students could be differentiated on bases other than their financial resources and preferences for working or borrowing. The borrowers were therefore asked whether they would favor the opportunity of increasing the amounts of their loans and the non-borrowers were asked to react to a potential liberalization of the federal insurance loan program.

Awareness of Loan Availability
and Attitudes toward Future

The borrowing and non-borrowing students demonstrated no significant differences with respect to either their knowledge of the availability of loans or the financial views of their futures. (These are considerations which might at least have conditioned the likelihood of initial interest in borrowing.)

A minority in both groups learned either from their high school guidance counselors or teachers of the availability of loans for trade and technical students. Only 21 percent of the non-borrowers had received such information. Even fewer of the borrowers — 17 percent

— had heard about loans from the source that should have been a prime one for such information. The connection between the awareness of available loans and borrowing is particularly suggestive (if not conclusive) when it is recalled that only 16 percent of all students were borrowers.

When student responses to this question were analyzed on the basis of enrollments in instructional programs, a maximum of 2 percentage points separated students in the ET and C&S programs. The highest percentage of students in any single group who had heard about loans totaled only 24 percent, and these were students in one term of the C&S program. Since the ET students usually have better high school records, it might be expected that they would uniformly have received more attention from counselors. Apparently this distinction simply does not apply; foremost attention is actually devoted to outstanding prospects for college and to even below average high school students in college preparatory programs.

Student responses to the following statement provide some measure of futuristic orientation and therefore are relevant to the propensity to borrow:

> The way things are now, I might as well buy what I want today and let tomorrow take care of itself.

Seventy-nine percent of the non-borrowing students and 73 percent of the borrowers disagreed strongly or somewhat with this statement. It would seem therefore that most of these students would be cautious regarding application for loans to finance their vocational education. At the same time, these students were presumably convinced that their futures could be meaningful. Such feelings may prevail among persons of lower- middle-income families who contemplate trying to secure a loan.

Borrowers' Interest in Increasing Size of their Loans

The students who were borrowers generally favored the opportunity to increase the amounts they had borrowed. Sixty-nine percent of the borrowers did, in fact, increase the size of their loans to $1,000 when the federal government raised the loan figure that it would insure.

The higher loan figure was, however, still insufficient to pay for annual tuition, books and supplies, which totaled about $1,500; and this is why most of the borrowers felt compelled to continue working. Hence 79 percent of the students who increased the amounts they were borrowing continued to hold jobs; and more than 70 percent of *all* borrowers still worked 20 or more hours weekly.

Thirty-five percent of the students who opted for higher loans indicated that their principal reason for working was to pay for a combination of such expenses as food, rent, clothing, family support and pocket money; only 8 percent of the students who did *not* take advantage of the increased amount that could be borrowed felt the same need ($p = .001$). Finally, the students who raised the amounts of their loans were more than 3 times as likely (as the students who did not) to list the loan as their major source of financial support. On the other hand, students who did not raise the amount borrowed were about 3 times as likely to specify employment as their major source of income.

The borrowing students were also asked whether they would borrow still more money if the government further increased the size of individual loans it would insure. Fifty-six percent of all borrowers (and 64 percent of those who had already raised their loans to the maximum) responded affirmatively. In addition, nearly 40 percent of the students who failed to take advantage of the previous maximum loan figure indicated they would be interested if the current maximum was increased. This is particularly noteworthy since most of these students said they would then stop working or reduce the number of hours they worked. Evidently, these students answered in the expectation that a considerably higher maximum loan would be established and, with that condition, they would become interested in borrowing more.

As shown in Table 8–7, the ET students in each term were considerably more desirous of borrowing greater amounts than the C&S students.

The students who expressed an interest in increasing their loans were then asked whether they would stop working or try to reduce the

TABLE 8–7

COMPARATIVE INTEREST OF ET AND C&S STUDENTS
IN INCREASING AMOUNTS BORROWED
IN PERCENTAGES, BY TERMS

Term	Program	Yes	No
1	ET	80%	20%
1	C&S	62	38
2	ET	63	38
2	C&S	45	55
3	ET	75	25
3	C&S	22	78
4	ET	50	50
4	C&S	17	83

$p = .001$ for students in Terms 3 and 4

number of hours they were working. Responses of these students follow:

Yes	No	Not Working
49%	48%	3%

Nearly all of these borrowing students were actually compelled to work; and they were about equally divided in their hypothetical intentions to stop working (or work less) or continue working. The students who answered they would neither stop working nor work less may have felt that an additional increase in the amount that could be borrowed would still fail to meet all of their financial responsibilities. Moreover, even if some students could meet all of their expenses from a larger loan (the amount of which was not specified in the question), they presumably would still not want to meet all of their obligations through borrowing.

Viewpoints of the Non-Borrowers

Table 8–8 shows the principal reasons why the non-borrowing students did not apply for a government-insured loan to finance their vocational educations. Thirty-five percent of the students indicated that their main reason for not borrowing was that they could rely upon their parents, or (to a much lesser extent) upon working spouses to finance their educations. (Forty-three percent of the non-borrowers in the ET program cited this reason as against 30 percent of the C&S students.) Another 10 percent of the respondents said they were counting upon the G.I. Bill or some form of state aid. Therefore, the remaining 55 percent depended upon income from employment. Half of the students who were working might actually have been interested in borrowing; but 4 percent could not secure a bank loan; 5 percent were not sure they would be able to repay a loan, and another 5 percent evidently felt the same way when they listed anticipated entrance into the military service as their reason for not borrowing; 14 percent of the students did not even know they could qualify for a loan.[10] This left only 27 percent of all non-borrowers who indicated they "would rather work and pay now than borrow and pay later."

The final question directed to the non-borrowing students was: "Would you take out a loan if the government not *only* paid most of the interest but also one-half the principal on your loan?" Only 30 per-

[10] The students who at the time of the questionnaire were still unaware of vocational education loans numbered considerably less than those who responded that they had not heard of the loans while in high school. Evidently the former group had not been reached by announcements on available loans issued each term by the RCA Institutes' administration. Of course, some of these students may have simply doubted (perhaps incorrectly) that they could qualify for loans.

TABLE 8–8

MAIN REASONS WHY NON-BORROWING STUDENTS DID NOT APPLY FOR A GOVERNMENT-INSURED LOAN, IN PERCENTAGES

	Prefer Working and Paying Now to Borrowing and Paying Later	Unable to Secure Loan from Bank(s)	Could Not Be Sure of Being Able to Pay Back Loan	Have Other Sources of Income (Parents, Spouse)	May Have to Enter Military Service After Graduation from School	Unaware of Being Able to Qualify for Loan	State Aid	G.I. Bill
Non-Borrowing Students	27%	4%	5%	35%	5%	14%	4%	6%

cent answered "No," and these "anti-borrowers" compare approximately with the 27 percent of all non-borrowers (shown in Table 8–8) who stated they would rather work than borrow. However, a special tabulation on the "anti-borrowers" disclosed that only 37 percent could be categorized as being in favor of working rather than borrowing even under very favorable terms. Another 46 percent were relying on the support of parents or spouses; and most of the remaining students depended on the G.I. Bill or various forms of state aid.

As the figures in Table 8–9 demonstrate, the ET students in every term were more likely than the C&S students to favor the above proposal on government loans, which is actually a partial-loan and partial-grant. Even so, the minimum C&S subgroup favoring the plan repre-

TABLE 8–9

NON-BORROWERS' POSITION ON PROPOSED PARTICIPATION IN LOAN-GRANT PLAN IN PERCENTAGES, BY TERM AND PROGRAM

Term	Program	Favor Participation	Do Not Favor Participation
1	ET	89%	11%
1	C&S	63	37
2	ET	75	25
2	C&S	68	32
3	ET	80	20
3	C&S	60	40
4	ET	77	23
4	C&S	74	26

$p = .001$ for the students in Terms 2 and 3

sented 60 percent of the students in the subgroup. It will be recalled that the C&S course typically requires less home study than the ET course; and therefore employment after school is comparatively feasible. Also, the C&S course is a half year shorter and less costly than the ET course; these would certainly be considerations regarding the interest in and need to borrow.

Although more than 43 percent of the ET students (in contrast to 30 percent for the C&S students[11]) said their main reason for not borrowing was the availability of support from parents or spouses, the attractive proposal made above caused a dramatic shift in favor of borrowing. The shift to a preference for borrowing may be due somewhat to the fact that financial aid from parents is treated as a form of no-interest "loan."

[11] The difference in percentages is significant at the .001 level.

Summary

A summation of the principal findings of this chapter is helpful in view of the several tables and numerical results presented. The typical student at RCA Institutes is undoubtedly very busy. His schooling and employment total 58 to 64 hours each week: he attends classes 25 hours and works an average of 22 hours after school; his hours of home study range from 11 to 17, depending upon his program. Students in the ET program average more hours of study than students in the C&S program. On the other hand, the rate of employment is higher for the C&S students and the rate increases over Terms 1–4; the opposite condition prevails for the ET students.

The borrowing students comprise 16 percent of all students and they are also more likely to work after school than the non-borrowers. All students who work do so out of necessity, in order to cover more than merely expenses for tuition and books.

Borrowing is the principal source of financial support for more than 40 percent of the borrowers. However, a question dealing with relative preferences for working and borrowing disclosed that 76 percent of the borrowers favor borrowing or a combination of borrowing and working to meet all of their expenses while attending school; only 47 percent of the non-borrowers indicate the same preference.

A majority of borrowers are interested in increasing the amount of their loans, even 40 percent of those who had not previously increased their loans to the maximum allowed. Apparently this 40 percent believe that a new maximum would be sufficiently high to meet all or most of their expenses. The ET students are much more likely to favor borrowing larger amounts than the C&S students.

The great majority of all non-borrowers would borrow to finance their schooling given more favorable terms. (Actually, nearly 30 percent of these students would have borrowed if they a) knew they could qualify for a loan; b) felt confident about repaying it; or c) had not been rejected for loans by banks. A separate question disclosed that 70 percent of the non-borrowers would take out a loan if the government paid most of the interest plus one-half of the principal on a loan.

CHAPTER 9

Performances of School Dropouts and High School Graduates in Private Vocational Schools

"... backward, dull, reluctant learners (whatever ugly or glamorous name is given them) ..."

— FRANKLIN J. KELLER, Principal
Emeritus, Metropolitan
Vocational High School,
New York

It was acknowledged previously that "disadvantaged" persons comprise a broad spectrum. Personal deficiency and financial deprivation are not the only causative factors; disadvantages may also be induced by conditions that fail to accommodate and reward the diverse interests and aptitudes of students.

Persons who are dropouts from primary and high schools (or, at times more accurately, "pushouts") are almost automatically disadvantaged when competing for jobs in the labor market. Yet many of these job-seekers stopped their formal education simply because available academic or vocational programs were unappealing to them; or else the schools were unable to accommodate their desire to switch from one instructional program to another.[1]

Some of these students have graduated from private vocational schools either immediately after leaving public school, following a spell of joblessness, or after disillusioning employment in an unchallenging occupation. Although the exact number of such school dropouts is not known, it is likely that they have accounted for at least one-third of the students enrolled in the private trade schools (excluding cosmetology,

---

[1] Nearly 25 percent of the school dropouts considered in this chapter quit school because they did not find their subjects interesting; and about 30 percent wᵉ forced to leave school in order to earn money.

barber and business schools) in recent years. On the basis of the estimated number of trade schools and students presented in Chapter 2, there were about 600,000 of these students each year.

This chapter attempts to ascertain — at least tentatively — how effectively school dropouts perform in competition with other students attending private vocational schools. Comparisons were made between a selected number of students[2] who were 1) high school graduates enrolled in trade schools, and 2) school dropouts enrolled in some of the same trade schools and courses. The students were evaluated, both while in training and in follow-up as job-holders, on the basis of the following considerations: personal traits,[3] financial resources and needs, program completion rates, job search, employment, relative satisfaction with jobs, and students' ratings of schools. The period covered was 1963–1966; the follow-up intervals were six months and one and one-half years.

The results presented here are based upon the data collected and tabulated through the Specialty Oriented Student Research Program at the University of Iowa. Professor Kenneth B. Hoyt is Director of the Program, which is concerned with the performances, problems and viewpoints of students enrolled in the private schools.[4]

Nearly all comparisons between the high school graduates and the school dropouts involved testing for association (usually with the chi-square test) between students' formal education level (fel) and numerous other factors.[5] Students were divided into the following three levels of schooling: 1) through the 9th grade; 2) past the tenth grade but not a high school graduate; 3) high school graduate. The school dropouts were about equally divided between fels 1) and 2), as seen in Table 9–1.

It seems natural to assume that the school dropouts were at some competitive disadvantage because of the higher educational attainments of the other trade students. Other data, moreover, disclosed that nearly 10 percent of the students in fel 3 had also attended college and some of these students could be called "college dropouts"; another

[2] No distinctions are made on the basis of sex. The females accounted for less than one percent of all students.

[3] The number of Negroes was not large enough to allow analysis as a distinct group. Moreover, a question on race was excluded in an early form of the SOS questionnaire.

[4] Appendix IV describes the Survey Procedures and lists limitations of the data.

[5] At times, a detailed frequency distribution or percentage can be presented only by utilizing data that differs by virtue of the presence of 14 dropouts in the category of trade students with a high school education. Since the dropouts represent less than 2 percent of a sizable number of students, it is unlikely that they cause much distortion.

TABLE 9–1

NUMBER OF STUDENTS ON THE BASIS OF
FORMAL EDUCATIONAL LEVEL (FEL)

FEL	*No. of Students*	*Percent of Students*
1) Finished 9th grade, but not 10th	65	5.9%
2) Finished 10th grade, but not 12th	63	5.7
3) High school graduate	977	88.4
	1,105	100.0%·

3 percent were actually graduates from a 4-year college or university.[6]

The relative rank of the fel 3 students in their high school classes is naturally a pertinent consideration. Seventy-seven percent of the trade students indicated they ranked in the second or third quarter of their graduating classes. This result can be considered quite *typical* for a large group of high school graduates.

Number of Students and Nature of Occupational Training

Table 9–2 shows the number of high school graduates and school dropouts enrolled in various types of occupational training.[7] More than 60 percent of the 1,105 trade students were enrolled in the auto mechanics course; the high school graduates were more likely to be represented in this course than the school dropouts, although more than 50 percent of the dropouts were enrolled in the same occupational training. The school dropouts, who represented 12 percent of all trade students, were somewhat more likely to be enrolled in the auto body-fender repair and machine operator courses than the high school graduates. In general, however, the two groups of students probably did not differ markedly on the basis of occupational training.

Comparisons of Age and Marital Status of Students

It will be illustrated that the school dropouts (hereafter referred to as dropouts) had obstacles to overcome other than their failure to

[6] In a group of more than 600 technical students (not considered here) 22 percent of the students had attended or graduated from a college or university.

[7] It was previously estimated that more than ⅓ of all trade and technical courses offered nationwide require less than high school graduation for admission. Table 9–1 shows a much smaller percentage of school dropouts for the following reasons: 1) the several schools in this survey are not representative of all schools; and 2) a general increase in the level of education has raised the qualifications of applicants for admission above a school's requirements.

TABLE 9–2

COMPARISON BETWEEN 1105 HIGH SCHOOL GRADUATES
AND SCHOOL DROPOUTS, BY TYPES OF OCCUPATIONAL TRAINING

Type of Occupational Training	Total No. of Students	Percent of all Students	No. of High School Graduates	Percent in each Course	No. of School Dropouts	Percent in each Course
Auto Mechanics	697	63.1%	630	64.5%	67	52.3%
Auto Body Fender Repair	91	8.2	74	7.6	17	13.3
Machine Operator	109	9.9	89	9.1	20	15.6
Other occupations including office machine repair, and refrigeration and air conditioning repair	208	18.8	184	18.8	24	18.8
	1,105	100.0%	977	100.0%	128	100.0%

complete high school. This group had more family responsibilities and was more limited in personal financial resources than the other trade students. For instance, most dropouts did not enroll in a private vocational school immediately after leaving school. This is documented by Table 9–3, which shows that there is a significant relationship between fel and age. However, the broad age breakdown fails to reveal how much older the average school dropout was than the high school graduate. Other data disclosed that 43 percent of the students in fels 1 and 2 were at least 25 years old; this was about three times the comparable figure for students in fel 3.[8]

The older age of the dropouts naturally implied greater family

TABLE 9–3

RELATIONSHIP BETWEEN FEL AND AGE OF TRADE STUDENTS

FEL	Under 21 Years of Age Number	Percent	Over 21 Years of Age Number	Percent
Fel 1	20	2.6%	45	14.0%
Fel 2	40	5.1	23	7.2
Fel 3	722	92.3	253	78.8
	783	100.0%	321	100.0%

Chi-square significant at .001 level

[8] The dropouts also had the highest percentage of students less than 18 years old, but they accounted for only 8 percent of the dropouts (as opposed to two percent for the high school graduates).

responsibilities. This was evident from the fact that only fel 1 had a majority of married students; and the percentage of married students in fel 2 were also higher than in fel 3. Altogether, 46 percent of the dropouts were married; this was nearly three times the rate found among the fel 3 students.[9]

There was no positive way of determining what effect age or marital status had upon performance. It has been suggested that older students find it more difficult to concentrate, but then World War II veterans attending college under the G.I. Bill of Rights were extremely serious and successful as a group. It could be expected that the interest and ambition of older students attending trade and technical school would also be high.

Financial Resources

About 60 percent of both the school dropouts and high school graduates acknowledged varying degrees of difficulty in financing their private vocational schooling. However, less than 15 percent of all the students were finding it "very hard" to finance their schooling; and only a very small percentage of students felt that financial constraints would make it impossible for them to complete their schooling.[10] Responses to this question could lead to the tentative conclusion that financial need was simply not great among this group of students. Therefore, of course, they could not be considered representative of persons who are *financially* hard-pressed or disadvantaged.[11] Actually, various "outside" (as well as personal) sources of money were available to the students.

There were important differences in the means of financing used by dropouts and high school graduates, and they are the most promising source for learning more about the financial position of the 1,105 trade school students considered here. The differences in the four sources of money, primarily nongovernmental, can be summarized as follows:

1. A majority of fels 1 and 2 (i.e., the school dropouts) did not use personal savings to pay their way through school; a slight majority of fel 3 (high school graduates) were using personal savings. (Chi-square significant at the .05 level.)
2. Whereas 43 percent of the parents of students in category fel 3 paid part of their schooling expenses, only 21 percent of fel 1 and 31 percent of fel 2 had this advantage. (Chi-square significant at .001 level.)

[9] The chi-square was significant at the .001 level.
[10] No significant relationship was found between fel and the financial difficulty students encountered.
[11] On the other hand, a minority of the students may have been especially motivated and confident of preparing for a meaningful occupational objective, and hence they minimized their financial need.

3. Although only a minority of all students had borrowed money from any source, approximately ¼ of fel 3 had borrowed and thereby exceeded the borrowing rate of dropout students by several percentage points.[12]
4. Fifty-one percent of the fel 3 students were employed as opposed to only 33 percent for fel 1 and 44 percent for fel 2. (Chi-square significant at .02 level.)

Significant associations are therefore disclosed between students' formal education level and recourse to personal savings, parents' assistance, loans and employment; the fel 3 students depended to a greater extent on all four sources of money to help defray their expenses than did the fel 1 and fel 2 students.

Since the school dropouts were on the average older and had more family responsibilities, it was surprising that less than 40 percent reported working to help "pay their way" through school. Another question, moreover, demonstrated that most of the fel 1 and fel 2 students had employment experience. Seventy-seven percent of the fel 1 students and 84 percent of the fel 2 students had held a full-time paid job (other than a summer position) at some time prior to entering trade school; in contrast, only 66 percent of the fel 3 students had previously worked full-time.[13] It is clear that the dropouts were less likely to be employed while they were students, despite their apparently greater financial needs and former full-time work experience.

The school dropouts were however greater beneficiaries of government aid, including mainly the programs of the Rehabilitation Services Administration and the Veterans Administration. As seen in Table 9–4,

TABLE 9–4

PERCENTAGES OF STUDENTS RECEIVING FINANCIAL AID FROM VOCATIONAL REHABILITATION AGENCY AND BUREAU OF INDIAN AFFAIRS

Government Programs	Percent of fel 1 and fel 2 receiving aid	Percent of fel 3 receiving aid
Vocational Rehabilitation Program	26.3%	6.0%
Bureau of Indian Affairs	3.0	.7
	29.3%	6.7%

[12] Students answered the following question: "Have you borrowed money from anyone to go to school?" The percentage of fel 3 students responding "yes" was 10 percentage points greater than for students at the RCA Institutes; there, however, students referred almost exclusively to loans received under the National Vocational Student Loan Insurance Act of 1965 (see Chapter 8).
[13] The chi-square was significant at the .01 level.

nearly 30 percent of the dropouts received financial assistance from either a Vocational Rehabilitation agency or the Bureau of Indian Affairs. This was four times the percent that obtained for the trade students who were high school graduates. In addition, 29 percent of the dropouts were veterans of military service, which was nearly twice as large as the figure for the fel 3 students. Presumably all (or at least a substantial proportion) of the veterans were utilizing the G.I. Bill of Rights while attending school.

In summary, although only 38 percent of the dropouts were employed while attending school, 58 percent were probably benefiting from various government programs; a total of 96 percent of these students were therefore either working or receiving some form of government aid. The combination of public aid programs plus employment applied to only 73 percent of the fel 3 students; of course, proportionately more of these students could depend on assistance from parents, savings and loans.

Comparative Course Lengths

The length of the courses in which students enrolled may be one measure of the comparative challenge of these courses. When courses were divided into periods of less than 15 months or more than 15 months, an association was shown between fel and course length (chi-square significant at .01 level). The fel 3 group had the highest percent enrolled in the longer courses but they accounted for only 14 percent of that group's students. Moreover, a finer breakdown disclosed that the dropouts had a higher percentage of students attending courses of at least 12 months in length than did the students who were high school graduates.[14]

Completion Rates and Additional Schooling

The relationship between fel and graduation rate from a course or program was significant (at the .01 level). Table 9–5 shows that the

TABLE 9–5

STUDENT GRADUATION RATES FROM PRIVATE VOCATIONAL SCHOOLS ON THE BASIS OF FORMAL EDUCATION LEVELS

FEL	*Percent Graduating*
Fel 1	78.5%
Fel 2	69.8
Fel 3	85.6

[14] The respective percentages were 29 and 27.

dropouts who had nine grades of schooling or less (fel 1) actually had a higher percent completing courses than the fel 2 students. This may have been due to the fact that the fel 1 group had more students enrolled in shorter or easier courses. Of course, the really impressive finding is that a high percentage of formal school dropouts did graduate from private vocational school programs; nearly ¾ of all school dropouts completed their program.[15]

A question dealing with additional schooling or training following departure from trade school revealed no statistically significant association with formal education levels. However, it is notable that 17 percent of all dropouts and 19 percent of the high school graduates enrolled for further schooling, mainly in another trade, technical or business school.[16]

At least two factors may explain why some students did not become "double dropouts." The fel 1 and fel 2 students worked less than the fel 3 students — evidently because they were much more likely to be recipients of government financial aid. They could therefore devote more time after school to review class or shop work. A second (and equally important) factor was that these students were highly motivated to succeed in the courses they had selected.

Period of Time for Beginning Job Search and Employment

No significant association was found between formal education levels and either the period of time that elapsed before the job search or the actual start of employment. Such findings are, of course, highly suggestive since they imply that students with different educational backgrounds displayed similar ambition in pursuing work and similar success in finding a job.[17]

More than 75 percent of each student group began looking for a job less than two weeks after leaving school. About ⅓ of all students had hardly any wait, because they had already been promised a job; and ⅔ of all students started looking for a job in less than one week.[18]

[15] Other data indicated that 14 percent of the school dropouts completed ¾ of the program in the private trade schools in contrast to 9 percent for the students who were high school graduates. Twelve percent of the dropouts and 6 percent of the high school graduates completed only ½ or less of their course.

[16] Three percent of the fel 3 students enrolled in a college or university; presumably 2 percent of the school dropouts who also enrolled had passed a high school equivalency test.

[17] The comparisons between school dropouts and high school graduates would have been still more meaningful if detailed occupational data were available.

[18] These students waited somewhat less time to begin their job search than a group of unemployed blue-collar workers in a study conducted during the summer of 1964. See Harold L. Sheppard and A. Harvey Belitsky, *The Job Hunt* (Baltimore: The Johns Hopkins Press, 1966), pp. 31, 32.

Four percent of both the dropouts and the high school graduates did not look for a job after leaving school.

As a result of their job search, 74 percent of the fel 3 students and 69 percent of the fel 1 and fel 2 students were employed within less than five weeks. Four percent of the high school graduates and 6 percent of the other students had not had a job since leaving school; but, as noted, some students enrolled for additional vocational schooling and even for college courses in certain cases.

There is a sizable discrepancy between the school placement ratios claimed by school officials (see Chapter 4) and the students' estimates shown in Table 9–6.[19] Less than 20 percent of the three categories of students had presumably first heard about the job they obtained from someone associated with the school. Another 10 percent

TABLE 9–6

SOURCES LEADING TO FIRST JOB FOR TRADE SCHOOL GRADUATES BY FORMAL EDUCATION LEVELS

FEL	School Official	Friends or Relatives	Newspaper or Magazine Ad	Employment Agency	Previous Employer
Fel 1	20.5%	38.5%	23.1%	12.8%	5.1%
Fel 2	14.3	38.1	14.3	16.7	16.7
Fel 3	19.6	53.0	7.4	9.7	10.3

of the students learned of their jobs through a previous employer; some students may have forgotten that the schools had been initially instrumental in their landing these jobs. Nevertheless, there is a significant relationship (at the .01 level) between the fel of the trade school students and the sources for learning about first jobs. More than a majority of the fel 3 group heard about their job from a friend or relative, compared with less than 40 percent of the fel 1 and fel 2 groups. The fel 1 and fel 2 groups were also more likely to depend on advertisements in newspapers or magazines and employment agencies; and although the use of these sources demonstrated creditable initiative, it is clear that these students could have benefited from greater assistance from the schools. Of course, since nearly 30 percent of the fel 1 and fel 2 students were sponsored under programs of the Rehabilitation Services Administration and the Bureau of Indian Affairs, their counselors may have provided some job leads.

A final consideration involves the distance from the training school to the site of the first job. The following figures show the relationship

[19] The school officials reporting in Chapter 4 did refer to a larger group of students than is considered in this chapter.

between fel and a distance of more than 100 miles between school and job:[20]

Fel 1	48.4%
Fel 2	55.7
Fel 3	70.2

Since 70 percent of the high school graduates and about 50 percent of the dropouts took jobs a considerable distance from their schools, it is further clarified why the schools were a comparatively less important source of job leads than friends or relatives and other sources.[21] Furthermore, more than 60 percent of the students who found employment over 100 miles from their school had ultimately returned to their home town.

Most of the remaining tests for association between formal education levels and other factors were not statistically significant. This may, of course, by itself be quite remarkable,[22] although additional interesting impressions and variations did occur within the three different groupings. The findings are therefore summarized.

Two examples include the students' views of the value of private vocational schooling. The first example deals with the way the former students would rate their school if questioned by a prospective student. Table 9–7 shows that at least 54 percent of each group rated their school very high to above average. Less than 15 percent of all students rated their schools below average to very low.

TABLE 9–7

FORMER STUDENTS' RATINGS OF PRIVATE VOCATIONAL SCHOOLS, BY EDUCATIONAL LEVELS

FEL	Very high to above average rating	Average Rating	Below average to very low rating
Fel 1	54.0%	30.2%	15.9%
Fel 2	65.6	26.2	8.2
Fel 3	53.9	34.5	11.6

[20] The chi-square test is significant at the .01 level.

[21] Many of the schools do however receive employer requests to place students in positions that are well over 100 miles from their schools.

[22] A comparison between disabled and non-disabled students also failed to show statistically significant relationships for some of the same factors considered here. The results are contained in *A Comparison of Characteristics, Educational and Vocational Experiences of Vocational Rehabilitation and Non-Vocational Rehabilitation Students in Selected Specialty Centers — A Plan for Study*, Kenneth B. Hoyt, Principal Investigator, Final Report for VRA Grant #RD-1536, June 29, 1965.

A second rather direct method of rating the schools was obtained by asking the former students whether their schooling helped them to do better on their first job. The answers were quite similar to those given in Table 9–7. Only 11 percent of the fel 1 group felt their schooling was not particularly helpful in their work; fel 2, with 20 percent, had the highest figure holding this view. These answers are also consistent with those given to another question dealing with the relevance of training to the first job after leaving school.

Nature of Job

Ninety percent of all students who secured jobs were working on a full-time basis. Of this group, high school graduates were only slightly more likely to have secured full-time work. The ratios of full-time employment were higher than those previously attained by each of the student groups; high school graduates had the largest percentage improvement — from 66 to 91 percent — but this would be mainly attributable to their being younger than the dropouts.

More than $\frac{4}{5}$ of all employed students were working in positions that were either equivalent or related to the types of training received.[23] This is an especially impressive result when considered in conjunction with the 12 percent of all employed students who said that they *did not* seek work in the area for which they were trained.

It is noteworthy that a majority of all students enjoyed their jobs primarily because of the type of skills and the variety of responsibilities involved in their work. Table 9–8 shows that 62 percent of the fel 3 group listed this combination of reasons, and this was a few percentage points more than for the school dropouts. Work surroundings were almost as important as the combination of earnings and job security for the fel 1 and fel 3 groups, but of considerably less importance to the fel 2 group.

No statistically significant relationship obtained between fel and earnings received on the first job after leaving school. Yet it was not feasible to compare the average earnings of all the trade students with another group that did not attend such schools, because insufficient data were available to account for differences due to geographical location, time of entrance into the labor market, and other considerations. However, among the three groups considered here, it is interesting that the fel 1 group had the *smallest* percentage of wage earners receiving less than $60 weekly.

[23] The individuals in fel 1 (i.e., those with less than 10 years of formal schooling) were somewhat more likely to find training-related jobs than persons in the other groups.

TABLE 9–8

WORKING CONDITIONS MOST FAVORED BY JOB-HOLDERS ACCORDING TO THEIR EDUCATIONAL BACKGROUNDS

FEL	Earnings	Kinds of job skills utilized	Chance to help other people	Prestige from the position	Work Surround-ings	Job Security	Working Associates	Variety of work
Fel 1	10.0%	38.3%	3.3%	3.3%	15.0%	6.7%	6.7%	16.7%
Fel 2	16.4	37.7	1.6	1.6	4.9	9.8	8.2	19.7
Fel 3	9.8	34.4	3.1	1.2	11.9	4.8	7.5	27.3

Job Satisfaction

About ⅔ of all persons employed in their first jobs after leaving school were either very satisfied or at least moderately satisfied with the work; the fel 1 group had the highest percent who were satisfied (see Table 9–9). Forty percent of the fel 2 group expressed varying

TABLE 9–9

**FORMER STUDENTS' SATISFACTION WITH FIRST JOB
BY FORMAL EDUCATION LEVELS**

FEL	Very satisfied or satisfied	Little dissatisfied	Quite or very dissatisfied
Fel 1	71.0%	12.9%	16.1%
Fel 2	60.0	23.3	16.7
Fel 3	66.0	20.4	13.6

degrees of dissatisfaction with their jobs, and the other two groups also had fairly sizable percentages of dissatisfied workers. Most of the dissatisfied persons also indicated they would (or already did) seek new work. Job dissatisfaction may reflect poor choice (or placement) of jobs, but it also may suggest that these trade student graduates were determined to find satisfying work. At the same time, when asked whether their jobs entailed the *type of work* which they could *not* do best only 15 percent or less were "quite certain" or "very certain" that it did.

Second Follow-Up of Former Students

For the most part, the second follow-up of all private trade school students also disclosed no significant relationship between formal educational level and employment status.[24] However, the size of the non-response rate was considerably larger than for the first follow-up questions.

Table 9–10 details the extent of job changes and the reasons for the changes. About half of the reporting persons were still employed in their first job. With the exception of about 10 percent of all former students who entered military service and another 10 percent who were laid off or fired, the remaining persons were either promoted and found better jobs or else left their jobs because they disliked their co-workers or working conditions. It is significant that 31 percent of the fel 2 group left their jobs for better positions in other companies,

[24] In a couple of instances, the number of cases within a cell were too small for the calculation of the chi-square; however the reported percentages (combining fel 1 and fel 2) are still of some interest.

TABLE 9–10

**EXTENT OF AND REASONS FOR JOB CHANGES
BY PREVIOUS EDUCATION LEVELS**

FEL	*Still on first job*	*Entrance into military service*[a]	*Promotion with company or found better job in another company*	*Dislike for work, or co-workers, or no chance for advancement*	*Laid off or fired*
Fel 1	54.0%	14.0%	14.0%	6.0%	12.0%
Fel 2	44.2	3.8	30.8	13.4	7.7
Fel 3	50.5	9.6	21.8	8.9	9.2

[a] A small percent left their jobs because a member of the family had secured a job in another community.

because this group was least satisfied with their first jobs (see Table 9–9). The fel 2 group were most likely to leave their first jobs because they disliked the work or their co-workers, or because there was no chance for advancement.

Relative Job Improvements

About 92 percent of the combined fel 1 and fel 2 groups held full-time jobs; 90 percent of the fel 3 group was employed full-time. This meant, at least on the basis of those reporting, that the second follow-up showed a slightly higher percent working full-time than the first follow-up.

Several questions were limited to those persons who had a full-time job before attending a trade school. They were asked to make comparisons between that job and the *first* job they secured after leaving school.

About ⅔ of each group answered that they were more satisfied with the job they took after their schooling. Only 5 percent of the combined fel 1 and fel 2 groups and 6 percent of the fel 3 group felt the new job left them worse off; the remainder found their satisfaction "about the same." A related question dealt with "the kinds of things done" on the two jobs. Approximately 70 percent of more than 400 respondents believed that their duties were "better now."

Nearly all former students were convinced that their schooling was helping them progress in their careers. Hence only two percent in each grouping said they were worse suited for the job acquired after schooling than for the one they had held previously. About ⅔ said they were better suited for the job secured after schooling and 30 percent reported being "about the same."

Table 9–11 shows no significant association between formal education level and changes in earnings on the two jobs. The comparative

TABLE 9–11

DIFFERENCES IN EARNINGS ON FULL-TIME JOBS
HELD BEFORE AND AFTER SCHOOLING
BY FORMAL EDUCATION LEVELS

FEL	Better now	About the same	Worse
Fel 1	55.6%	22.2%	22.2%
Fel 2	65.9	20.5	13.6
Fel 3	62.1	26.3	11.7

advances in earnings were several percentage points less than the general, non-quantifiable improvements cited for the jobs in the two different time periods; this was particularly true for the group with the least formal education (fel 1).

Earnings for all new jobs would not necessarily be greater than for those previously held merely because the new jobs required training. The opportunity for advancement in the new jobs, not earnings per se, is the prime consideration. Responses to two other questions confirm this. Most of the persons in the fel 1 group who reported a decline in earnings also maintained that their chances for job stability and promotion had improved.[25]

[25] An additional influence might have been the fact that 26% of the persons in the fel 1 and 2 groups were recipients of Vocational Rehabilitation grants and some of them might have been forced into new occupations by serious diseases or injuries.

CHAPTER 10

Adaptation of Private and Public
Programs to the Disadvantaged

"The training of the disadvantaged clearly presents an entirely new labor market challenge for the traditional vocational system . . . this is a challenge still to be faced."
— PROFESSOR GERALD SOMERS[1]

Earlier chapters have demonstrated the partial utilization of private vocational schools for training disadvantaged persons and others who seek the most expeditious means of entering full-time work. The schools have been largely ignored thus far by educators and counselors, who have been primarily concerned with preparing and placing their students in colleges and universities. It is ironic that, at the same time, many of the training measures long practiced by the private schools have gained prominence recently as effective "innovations" for motivating and instructing persons with various handicaps.

It was estimated that, as a group, the proprietary trade and technical schools are operating profitably, even though they are operating at only about 60 percent of both their feasible and optimum capacity.

This chapter recommends a fuller utilization of the private schools' training resources. Principal attention is focused upon ways of increasing the opportunities of persons interested in enrolling in the private schools. The result can best be achieved by changes or expansions in existing government-aided programs and the initiation of new programs. Joint public-private training ventures are believed to offer exceptional scope for improving the positions of both public and private organizations; but, most important of all, the alternatives of students and unemployed or underemployed persons can be enhanced thereby.

---

[1] From his article, "The Response of Vocational Education to Labor Market Changes," in *Vocational Education*, Supplement to the Journal of Human Resources, Vol. III, 1968, p. 37.

Brief Review of the
Schools' Training Advantages

Specific training (or training for limited occupational objectives) within a job-simulated setting characterizes the programs of private vocational schools. Students are nevertheless offered the opportunity at many of the schools to train for different occupations or different skill levels within an occupation. For example, a student who is enrolled in an electronics technician course may decide that he prefers another but still related course, for any of several reasons, including degree of interest, talent, ambition or financial security. The school is likely to have a shorter and even more applied course in the servicing of radio and television and the student can often transfer to such a course. Some schools offer such varied programs that they can even accommodate the student who decides that he actually prefers to train for a completely different occupation.

The schools' course materials are presented in small achievement units and they are therefore rather easy to assimilate; and the "rewards" (some form of recognition or grade) occur more often than in most general education courses. This form of instruction has proven successful with school dropouts and other disadvantaged persons who were not stimulated by general education subjects.

Many courses in the private vocational schools are highly individualized. This can be attributed, in certain courses, to the fact that the rates of progress by individual students differ markedly; the schools have therefore made adjustments to different needs and capacities of students.

The instructors are expected to successfully motivate and train a high percentage of their students. Since most students work part-time, instructors are required to make course materials comprehensible through vivid presentations and demonstrations in the classrooms, shops and laboratories so that homework can be kept to a minimum. Remedial courses, review sessions after school hours, and other aids are available for students encountering difficulties with their courses.

Although several of the desirable features in the instructional programs of private vocational schools have been emulated by some public school systems, it is clear, for numerous reasons, that the proprietary schools will remain viable. In the first place, the private schools often complement public school facilities which are alone inadequate to serve the entire community's demand. Then again, the two systems may provide some of the benefits claimed for any form of competition. Moreover, there are often differences in the content of instruction; the private schools teach only those elements of basic education necessary for the performance of the ultimate occupation or skill, while the public vocational schools are likely to include general education materials in their programs.

In any case, a plan that contemplates expansion of the public facilities must reckon with two major costs: a) the expense of adding the new vocational programs; and b) the possible social waste of unutilized or underutilized private facilities.[2] At present, many private vocational schools operate virtually side-by-side with free tuition schools. The former have often been preferred by students because their training programs are more intensively job-oriented. Therefore, attempts to substitute public training for all of the privately provided training would undoubtedly lead to underutilization in both the public and private schools.

A second reason for continuing viability of the private schools concerns certain of their unique course offerings which could be provided in the public schools only at prohibitive costs. Such highly specialized courses as diamond-setting, dog grooming, meat cutting, time-study engineering and numerous others are of comparatively short duration or would be difficult to integrate into the public school programs. The private schools have also established programs that often enroll only a small number of students at any given time. The schools can profitably offer these courses because they enroll students several times during the year and their training year is practically equivalent to the calendar year; these schools also attract students from other communities, states and even foreign countries, who will return to their homes after completing the training.

In the third place, private schools have the advantage of early experimentation with "new" programs and innovation in methods of instruction and course materials. Their experimentation may be expected to continue as a result of the schools' close ties with business firms and the incentive to maximize profits.

Private Schools' Participation in Government Programs

Private vocational schools — usually indirectly through their students — have participated in a number of government training programs. Only one out of the 128 responding NATTS schools had never been involved in at least one program sponsored by the federal government,

[2] The Iowa Legislature has tried to avoid duplication in the State's total vocational education resources. An amendment to the Iowa Area Vocational School Bill provides that a curriculum will not be approved unless "all courses and programs submitted for approval are needed and that the curriculum being offered by an area school does not duplicate programs provided by existing public or private facilities in the area."

a state government or by both governments. Table 10–1 shows that nearly every school has trained students under both the Veterans and Vocational Rehabilitation programs. The private schools and their students have, however, benefited considerably less under several of the newer governmental programs, including those sponsored by the

TABLE 10–1

PARTICIPATION IN FEDERAL OR STATE TRAINING PROGRAMS
BY NATTS SCHOOLS

Program or Sponsoring Agency	No. of Schools	Percent of Schools
Veterans Administration	126	98.4%
Vocational Rehabilitation	123	96.1
Manpower Development and Training	83	64.8
Immigration and Naturalization Service[a]	70	54.7
Office of Economic Opportunity	50	39.1
National Vocational Student Loan Insurance	42	32.8
Indian Affairs	36	28.1
Other	28	21.9

[a] This agency approves schools for attendance by nonimmigrant students, but it does not make any payments to students.

Office of Economic Opportunity. The "other" category is comprised mainly of students who qualify under the federal programs of Aid to Dependent Children and Refugee Assistance; two schools have trained persons for the Agency for International Development and a few schools listed state scholarships for which their students have qualified.

Disparities in the use of private vocational schools under various public programs clearly imply that the schools' capabilities for successfully preparing persons for work have not been adequately appreciated. There has been obvious underutilization of the schools, which are both able and willing to train many more persons than those currently enrolled.

It was estimated in Chapter 3 that more than ½ million additional students could be accommodated in the existing facilities of the nation's trade and technical schools.[3] Invariably, moreover, the school owners favor those government programs that would benefit students directly either through loans or grants. Only five out of 104 responding schools preferred direct payments or subsidies to the schools.[4]

[3] This estimate *excludes* the 4,000 schools of business, cosmetology and barbering.
[4] A couple of these school owners recommended the supplying of surplus government equipment to private schools under the same favorable conditions available to public agencies.

The member schools of NATTS indicated that they were especially anxious to provide more training in afternoon classes; many schools were also prepared to enroll more students in morning and evening sessions. In addition, although most schools operate on a year-round basis, the capacity to expand enrollments is greater during the summer months.

Although a scientific estimate is lacking, several million persons could surely gain from occupational training. The number of people eligible for vocational rehabilitation services *alone* has been estimated at four to six million by the Rehabilitation Services Administration; eligibility under this program requires certification of potential employability. Yet, less than ¾ million people were served by the program in the fiscal year 1968.[5]

As noted previously, the Vocational Rehabilitation programs in most states have depended heavily upon the training resources in private vocational schools.[6] Since individual referrals can be made at frequent intervals, the schools can make prompt decisions on applications from persons who are disabled by a variety of diseases and injuries. Moreover, the operating agencies within the states employ qualified counselors who are concerned with the placement of disabled persons in the most ideal training setting. The counselors carefully follow the progress of the trainees and are also active in the trainees' job search and placement.

Manpower Development and Training Act (MDTA)

Most of the contracts awarded under this program provide much less counseling by a public body than is the practice with the Vocational Rehabilitation Program. The informal counseling available in most private schools may therefore be useful. Job placement under this program is the responsibility of the U. S. Employment Service.

There has been a very uneven use of proprietary schools in training unemployed and underemployed persons under the MDTA. More than 50 percent of the training in Chicago has been provided by the private schools. The State of New York has awarded only about 15 percent of the program's training to these schools, and practically all of the contracts have been individual referrals rather than contracts for entire classes of students; once again the schools demonstrate,

---

[5] Garth L. Mangum and Lowell M. Glenn, *Vocational Rehabilitation and Federal Manpower Policy* (Institute of Industrial and Labor Relations, University of Michigan and Wayne State University, Nov. 1967), p. 18.

[6] According to one estimate approximately half of the training financed under these programs was done in private schools.

through their open-end curricula, the capacity to accommodate individual students from different (and often distant) communities within the state and during several periods of the school year.

On a national basis, according to estimates by the Department of Health, Education and Welfare, the use of private vocational schools has been steadily increasing. The schools were expected to account for about 20 percent of all institutional training under MDTA in 1968.[7] Sixty-five percent of the reporting NATTS members indicated they had done some training under the MDTA. However, only a small number of schools considered the program an important source of students.

It is appropriate to consider some of the attempts by Congress and federal agencies to expand the utilization of private schools under MDTA because of their pertinence to other legislation that could involve the schools — in particular the Vocational Education Act of 1963 and its Amendments.

Initially, the states were given the option of utilizing either proprietary schools or the public facilities for training persons under the MDTA. Since this proved rather ineffective (the private schools were still underutilized), Congress legislated the requirement that the schools *would* be utilized if the quality of their course offerings matched those available in any public facility and the training could be provided at a lower cost. Some states still ignored the private schools, arguing that state funds could not legally be used to aid proprietary education.[8] This moved the Congress to revise the Act so that under some conditions states could waive a 10 percent matching contribution when utilizing private schools.[9]

Opposition to the use of proprietary schools under the MDTA has persisted despite their frequent ability to underbid the public schools when vying for contracts.[10] It is claimed that the private schools were, at times, not awarded contracts because the public schools wished to expand their own training activities. This was done by applying for

[7] The percent refers to dollar outlays. The percent of students in training is less because most of the training is accomplished through individual referrals.

[8] Some states also claimed that it would be contrary to the legislation for them to place contracts in schools offering less than the prescribed number of weekly instructional hours. Certain private schools adjusted by offering extra student help after regular school hours.

[9] Actually, the U. S. Office of Education must decide whether or not to waive the 10 percent matching amount. At times, private schools have reduced their tuitions by 10 percent or less, but the full matching figure has been waived in many instances.

[10] An administrative official in the education department of a large and populous state said the private schools have invariably won contracts when competing with the public schools.

MDTA funds to perform minor remodeling of existing space and to purchase required equipment. Such expansions may have resulted in some duplication (and even eventual underutilization) of facilities because the resources available in the private schools were not carefully assessed.[11] A more common (but perhaps related) charge has been that private school facilities were unfairly declared unacceptable by state vocational education directors.[12] Although officials in Washington have been sympathetic at times, they have not considered it feasible to send federal representatives to investigate a substantial number of questionable situations. For one thing, this would lead state officials to develop effective defenses against federal incursions. Still, an undesirable situation has been created: many schools that have reputedly been treated unfairly have simply refrained from entering additional bids for MDTA contracts. If worthwhile competition is replaced by a virtually monopolistic situation, the result can be inefficiency in the use of extremely scarce training resources. (It would naturally not make much difference whether the monopolist was a public education agency or the owner of proprietary schools.)

The U. S. Department of Health, Education and Welfare made a meaningful response to the charge of comparative neglect of private vocational schools by awarding a national contract on a "pilot" basis directly to the United Business Schools Association (UBSA) in February 1967. One of the criteria for selection of schools under the contract was that they either be located in states where the private schools had been utilized only minimally, or else the individual referral system had been used only infrequently.[13] The principal objectives were

. . . to simplify and speed up the procedures for referring individuals for private school training, to expand use of private schools in Manpower Training and to ascertain the ability of these institutions to serve disadvantaged persons.[14]

[11] The proportion of MDTA funds assigned for remodeling and purchase of equipment has declined steadily from about 26 percent to 3 percent of total outlays. Moreover, the equipment remains the property of the federal government and it can be moved to public schools, even in another state, when this is considered desirable.

[12] A federal government official observed that state and local educational authorities have established patterns of operation and they have a "community of interest." He said this is a condition in most institutional settings. In addition, the private schools are often considered unproven by government educators. Of course, they may be "unproven" because the public educators have not tried to learn what private vocational schools can do.

[13] The individual referral method is of course a hallmark of the private vocational schools' training.

[14] Report of the Secretary of Health, Education and Welfare to the Congress on the Manpower Development and Training Act, 1967, p. 27.

The contract enabled UBSA to make agreements with interested schools in the Association; NATTS was designated as a subcontractor for training in non-business occupations. The schools worked directly with the local offices of the U. S. Employment Service, which did the recruiting, selecting and referring of trainees on the basis of counseling and testing.

The original contract with UBSA, which applied to schools in eight states, was amended and extended through June 30, 1969. Whereas the contract's first phase provided only for vocational training, the second phase included provisions for remedial work in basic education and cooperative work-study arrangements; and more than 50 schools in 10 different states were involved in the second phase of the contract.[15]

Early indications supported the long-time claims by the private schools concerning their capabilities for motivating and training disadvantaged persons through the method of individual referrals. In general, it was found beneficial to combine the unemployed trainees (who were referred either individually or in small groups) with the more typical, highly motivated students attending the schools; and, at times, teachers were even unaware which students were "disadvantaged," i.e., enrolled under MDTA auspices. At least one school had contracts for training an entire class of students sponsored by the MDTA and a class with several individual referrals plus regular paying students; combining individual referrals with the regularly enrolled students, who have been called "self starters," is considered the superior way to train persons under the MDTA.[16]

It seems that a government contract with a national association (such as UBSA or NATTS) can be an effective means for allocating training funds.[17] Therefore the national associations of private vocational schools (which also have accrediting bodies that are recognized by the U. S. Office of Education) deserve consideration for additional contracts of this type.

However, nationwide contracts that can be allocated expeditiously will certainly not be ideal under all circumstances. Although such contracts provide the potential opportunity for private vocational schools to work in concert with the local offices of the Employment

[15] Some schools informally provided remedial instruction and orientation to employment, when needed, in the contract's first phase.

[16] Although the paper work required of the schools participating in the pilot program was less than average, it was still felt by some school owners that an entire class of MDTA trainees was preferable to individual referrals from purely administrative and financial viewpoints.

[17] Similar direct contracts have in fact been the major way of utilizing other types of private resources under the MDTA.

Service, state and local education officials are *bypassed*. The few instances of joint effort between public and private schools are encouraging but the practice must be generalized.

Expansion of Public-Private Training Arrangements

The 1968 Amendments to the Vocational Education Act provide state boards of education with the authority to contract for training in accredited private vocational schools. The amendments, passed five years after enactment of the 1963 Act, contain no mandates to the state boards of education. That is, although private schools are specifically mentioned, contracts with the school will be at the *discretion* of the states.

The potential yield of joint public-private ventures in vocational education can be optimistically contemplated. The number of persons who could benefit from occupational training is virtually unlimited; and training can be provided both for high school students and for persons who dropped out of school or were merely not prepared for worthwhile employment. In view of their varied backgrounds, abilities and interests, the challenges for preparing people for employment would involve more than skill training. Vast improvements must be effected even in basic education. Supplementary services would include remedial education, counseling and work orientation.

Joint public-private ventures could satisfy the interests of many high school students, and even some of the older students enrolled in junior high schools. A direct result would be the elevation of students' enthusiasm and accomplishments. The cooperative arrangements would also improve the over-all performances of both systems of schooling; and this upgrading would in turn produce additional benefits for the students.

Unlike the private vocational schools, most public schools are often constrained by both their structural organization and their objectives. Whereas the administrative decisions of a proprietary school are made by a single director or a small group, several departments of a local government must be involved in the purchase of a piece of equipment for a public school located in a large city.[18] Actually, delays may be present at an earlier stage, because a local school board may act only at its regular monthly meeting, for example, the third Thursday of every month; and the board may have to allow for open bidding before any new equipment can be purchased. The school boards have them-

---

[18] It has been decided in court cases that a public school superintendent usually cannot make administrative decisions without consulting the school board.

selves been saddled by conflicting demands and expectations of articulate critics within their communities. Finally, the boards have been mainly composed of professional, business and religious leaders who have tended to both separate general and vocational education and devote principal attention to the former.[19]

Dr. Walter Arnold, a former Assistant Commissioner for Vocational and Technical Education in the U. S. Office of Education, has observed that the public schools are "literally boxed-in." The schools and their students are expected to fit into a *pattern;* otherwise either the school or the student is declared a failure. Given this necessity, the schools have then been inconsistently criticized for failing to take care of individual problems among their students.

As illustrated previously, the private vocational schools are very different from most public schools. The private schools can readily adapt to sudden changes in the needs of students and employers. Adjustments in schedules or courses can be aligned with what are virtually *individual* requirements of students and employers.[20] One of the most salient distinctions between the two school systems concerns their respective capabilities for making innovations in their instructional programs. A Professor of Education at the University of the City of Los Angeles has concluded:

> The role of the proprietary and nonprofit institution in vocational education is vital to the success of vocational education as a whole . . . public agencies, through no fault of their own, do tend to be behind the times.[21]

The flexibility of the private schools' operations would enable them to accommodate students both during the normal school year and the summer months. Since the afternoon sessions are not fully utilized they could be an appropriate time for the public schools to initiate training contracts with the private schools. Numerous schools would, however, also be able to accept high school students during morning or evening sessions whenever that proved more convenient for the

[19] "Researchers at the Battelle Memorial Institute have surveyed school boards in Ohio and concluded that most do not know what kind of education the public wants or needs and that even if the boards did, they would not know whether they were providing it." See *The New York Times,* July 18, 1968.

[20] H. V. Kincaid and E. A. Podesta have raised the question of whether ". . . proprietary schools represent a potential for expansion of the public school vocational programs — particularly in areas of short-term need or modest student demand . . ." See "An Exploratory Survey of Proprietary Vocational Schools," in Quirk and Sheehan (eds.), *Research in Vocational and Technical Education* (Madison: The Univ. of Wisconsin, 1967), p. 222.

[21] Claude W. Fawcett, "Responsibilities of Non-Public Agencies for Conducting Vocational Education," in *Vocational Education,* 64th Yearbook of the National Society for the Study of Education (Chicago: University Press, 1965), p. 257.

public schools or their students. Summer programs could be arranged so that the reputed benefits of year-round school attendance could be realized by some students.

The 1968 Amendments to the Higher Education Act would, moreover, enable proprietary schools to participate in the National Defense Student Loan Program and the College Work-Study Program. Under the first program, needy students who are unable to secure bank loans would be able to borrow from the federal government funds allocated to the private schools. The Work-Study Program would permit students to work up to fifteen hours per week in public or private nonprofit institutions. It has been noted that "the purpose of work-study is income; that of cooperative work-experience programs is to couple training in the school and on-the-job." [22] Professor Mangum's view that the number of "work-experience" programs should be maximized is generally sound. Of course, the greater usage of private vocational schools in joint public-private programs would per se yield major improvements over the previous education that many young persons have found sterile, because the instructional content and setting in the private schools do approximate ultimate job experiences.

As suggested before, the widespread implementation of the section of the Vocational Education Act dealing with private vocational schools could have substantial influences upon the public schools and their students. The many and often conflicting demands that have been levied upon the public schools would probably be eased. A prime benefit ought to be the schools' opportunities for reassertion as the outstanding resource for transmitting the basics of education. Since persons do differ in their abilities to learn, it will always be challenge enough to provide all persons with the best possible general education they are capable of mastering. Certainly a solid general education is a requirement for most students enrolling in private vocational schools.[23] Cases were cited earlier in which school owners, teachers and students reported low achievement in mathematics, English and other subjects. As students become better prepared in the high schools, private vocational schools could raise the level of sophistication for many of their courses.

[22] Garth L. Mangum, *Reorienting Vocational Education,* A Joint Publication of the Institute of Labor and Industrial Relations, University of Michigan, and Wayne State University, May 1968, p. 17.

[23] In addition to preparatory programs for students planning to attend colleges or universities, Dr. James B. Conant favors an ample general education for all high school students and ". . . good elective programs for those who wish to use their acquired skills immediately after graduation." See *The Comprehensive High School* (New York: McGraw-Hill Book Co., 1967), p. 23. It is suggested here that joint public-private ventures would generate opportunities for many students which are unavailable in most public vocational schools.

The beneficial impacts of joint public-private programs upon participating high school students cannot be proven directly, but some of the highly likely effects can be inferred from certain experiences. For example, high school dropouts are accepted by many of the private vocational schools, and, as shown in Chapter 9, their performances while in school and upon graduation are not substantially different from those of the students who had graduated from high school. It can be safely assumed that many of the dropouts from public schools had encountered academic difficulties or else they were not stimulated by the course offerings;[24] and at least some of the students must have translated their disappointments into behavior that teachers simply treated as disciplinary problems. With proper interest and motivation these problems were evidently absent in the private vocational schools.

It is quite probable that similar results would ensue from joint public-private ventures that state boards of education will have the opportunity to promote under the amended Vocational Education Act. Many of the high school students who will also enroll in proprietary schools for part of each day may react more positively to regular schooling. In the first place, their vocational interests will not be thwarted any longer. Secondly, the interrelationships between the general and practical forms of schooling may be more fully understood and appreciated. One of the net results could be a lower dropout rate in the high schools.

Several state laws allow "early school leavers" to work part-time and attend school part-time.[25] Early school-leaving should naturally not be encouraged, but among some of the individuals for whom it is advisable, a combination of private vocational schooling and part-time work might prove successful. However, work-experience programs for these young persons cannot be tried in many states unless there are legal and administrative changes in the compulsory school attendance and child labor laws.

Opportunities for Out-of-School Persons

It is not known what percentage of persons who have been students in private vocational schools could be considered "disadvantaged." However, there is no doubt that many of the disadvantaged who could

---

[24] A doctoral dissertation on vocational education in the U. S. disclosed that most programs contained a limited number and variety of occupational courses. Comparatively few courses were available for "low ability students," and courses were mainly offered to eleventh and twelfth grade students. Overall it was felt "the number of students enrolled is unrealistically low." See Joseph L. McCleary, *Vocational Education Programs Offered in the Metropolitan Public High Schools of the United States* (Univ. of So. Calif. Sch. of Ed., 1967).

[25] See Harold T. Smith, *Education and Training for the World of Work* (Kalamazoo, Mich.: The W. E. Upjohn Institute for Employment Research, July 1963), p. 39.

benefit from job-oriented instruction have not been enrolled in such schools.

As shown before, several factors have impeded the greater utilization of private schools. To a considerable extent obstacles have centered around such matters as student motivation and educational values. A broad definition of disadvantaged (but a defensible one) could include those high school graduates of a college preparatory program who lack either interest or ability for college study and are also unprepared vocationally. All too often, however, information on the opportunities available through private schools has been denied to high school students because the public school counselors have had excessive counseling loads, while also directing most of their attention to college-bound youths; in any case the counselors' knowledge of the labor market and vocational schools has been too limited.

Even when high school graduates or dropouts are aware of the programs offered in private vocational schools and also eager to be enrolled, they may of course lack the financial resources to attend. Some of the more recent MDTA programs and also those financed under the Economic Opportunity Act have attempted to aid these people, but these programs (especially MDTA) also accommodate the education and training needs of older age groups; and at times special emphasis has been placed upon unemployed and underemployed persons — i.e., those who have established attachment to the labor force. Many young persons serving in the armed forces, at least during periods of armed conflict, will probably continue to have the opportunity to qualify for the G.I. Bill of Rights. Certain distinct groups (Indians, the physically and emotionally handicapped and public assistance recipients, among others) will also undoubtedly receive special attention.

At this time, the funds of 20 federal programs are available to proprietary schools either through a contract relationship between a school and the government or through financial aid to students enrolled in the schools. The various programs which are shown in Table 10–2 are about equally divided between 1) "under contract" training and 2) student financial grants, loans or tax benefits.

The multiplicity (or, according to some, the pluralism) that has often characterized government programs in other fields will continue to exist with education and training programs. This condition has been derided, often mistakenly, because of excessive costs of administration attributable to overlapping and even duplicating programs. Of course, the absence of single solutions to training and other challenges represents practical political adjustments that may even be (naturally not always wittingly) intelligent responses to problems that cannot be treated uniformly. Also, any additional costs of multiple

TABLE 10–2

FEDERAL GOVERNMENT PROGRAMS PERMITTING
PRIVATE VOCATIONAL SCHOOL PARTICIPATION

"Under Contract" Training

1. Vocational Rehabilitation Act of June 2, 1920, as amended 29 U.S.C. 31 *et seq.*
2. Manpower Development and Training Act of 1962, as amended, 42 U.S.C. 2571; P.L. 89–792.
3. Indian Adult Vocational Education; 25 U.S.C. 309, 452, 823 (c).
4. Economic Opportunity Act of 1964, as amended, 42 U.S.C. 2701 *et seq;* P.L. 89–794.
5. Government Employee's Training Program; P.L. 89–554; 5 U.S.C. 4101–4118.
6. Economic Development Administration (P.L. 89–15) 42 U.S.C. 2583.
7. Vocational Education Act of 1963; P.L. 88–210; Sec. 8 (1).
8. Veteran's Vocational Rehabilitation; 38 U.S.C. 1501–1511.
9. Social Security Amendments Act of 1967 (P.L. 90–248) Title II Public Welfare Work Training Programs.

Student Financial Grants, Loans or Tax Benefits

10. Social Security Student Dependents, P.L. 89–97; See Sec. 202 (d) (8) (C).
11. F.E.C.A. Student Dependents; P.L. 89–488; See Sec. 10 (M).
12. Railroad Retirement Student Dependents; P.L. 89–700; See Sec. 5 (1) (I).
13. Civil Service Retirement Student Dependents; 5 U.S.C. 2251–2268; See Sec. 2251 (j) and Sec. 2260, and P.L. 89–504; 5 U.S.C. 89–554; Sec. 8341.
14. War Orphans Educational Assistance; 38 U.S.C. 1701 *et seq.*
15. Veterans Readjustment Benefits Act of 1966; P.L. 89–358; See Sec. 1652 (c).
16. Vocational Loans to Indians; 25 U.S.C. 471.
17. Vocational Loans to Eskimos; 25 U.S.C. 479.
18. National Vocational Student Loan Insurance; P.L. 89–287.
19. Income Tax Deduction for Student Dependents; 26 U.S.C. 151 (e) (4).
20. Student Dependency and Indemnity Compensation for Veterans Children; 38 U.S.C. 104, 414 (c).

Source: Statement by William Elkins in: U. S. Congress, House, Committee on Education and Labor, *Partnership for Learning and Earning Act of 1968, Hearings,* before the General Subcommittee on Education, on H.R. 15066, 90th Cong., 2nd Sess., 1968, pp. 345–346.

training programs may be at least partly compensated for through the benefits of trying somewhat different training techniques.[26] In any case, a variety of responses to social and educational challenges appears to be a persistent reality.

Needed: Liberalized Student Loans

The National Vocational Student Loan Insurance Act (NVSLIA), one of the most recent and promising programs aimed at helping students to finance their training, has for several reasons failed to meet

---

[26] The usefulness of different training techniques is of course dependent upon the effective communication and application of the results wherever relevant.

expectations.[27] The financial opportunities available under the Act have not been revealed to most prospective students of private vocational schools;[28] and even had they known about the Act their chances of borrowing funds would not have been good. As explained earlier, college-bound students would be more successful in securing loans than the vocational school students, especially if the insured or guaranteed loan fund provided by the federal government remains comparatively limited.[29]

Even when the volume of loans that the government *would* insure under the NVSLIA is increased appreciably, the willingness of private banks to extend credit to potential borrowers will remain as the ultimate determinant of the program's success. Thus far, several private vocational school owners have reported that most banks do not participate at all under the loan program while some banks are only minimally involved and an exceptionally small number of banks make most of the loans.[30] The most common complaints of non-participating banks are the low rate of return on educational loans and the related objection to tying up funds for long periods of time.

The interest rate on loans under the NVSLIA was increased from 6 to 7 percent effective August 1968. A higher rate of interest plus effective counseling of high school students on the advantages of credit would undoubtedly increase the amount of borrowing to finance vocational education.[31] As shown previously (p. 109), more than 50 percent of all first-year students at RCA Institutes favored either borrowing or the combination of borrowing and working to meet all of their expenses. Since most students at the school hold part-time jobs (aver-

---

[27] Only a small part of the fault can be placed with the administrators of the Act who were cautious in implementing it. The administrators indicated they were carefully attempting to avoid some of the weaknesses in the application of the college student loan program.

[28] Only a small percentage of students attending RCA Institutes in New York City had heard of the Student Loan Insurance Act from high school counselors or teachers (see pp. 109–110).

[29] United Student Aid Funds (USAF), a private nonprofit corporation serving higher education, had guaranteed more than 2,600 loans to students attending vocational schools during 1967. It was expected that this admirable record would be doubled in 1968. William J. Davis, Vice President of USAF, wrote: "The guaranteed loan program does afford, we think, a unique opportunity for disadvantaged youngsters to gain a vocational education."

[30] Prospective borrowers who live in large metropolitan areas may encounter greater difficulty in securing loans than persons living in small towns. The banks in the larger cities tend to have investments with higher earning potentials; and such banks are usually not as intimate with most personal depositors as are the banks in small communities.

[31] Nearly 30 percent of the non-borrowing students at RCA Institutes were either unaware of loan availability, unsure of being able to qualify for loans, or unsuccessful in securing bank loans (see p. 113).

aging 22 hours weekly), the typical student devotes about 60 hours weekly to school attendance, employment and study at home. Only 10 percent of the students were employed because they found the work enjoyable or because it was related to their course; financial need was therefore the primary reason for working. At the same time, most of these students, and also the major portion of the students who have attended private vocational schools, have definitely *not* included the most economically disadvantaged persons in the population. Thus less than 15 percent of the 1,105 students considered in Chapter 9 said they were finding it "very hard" to finance their schooling.[32]

It is still important to take account of the need for most students in private vocational schools to work, even though only a rather small percentage of the students have found it *extremely* difficult to finance their schooling. Many schools have adapted their instructional programs so that required home study is kept to a minimum. The highly practical content of the typical course necessitates per se the accomplishment of a major portion of classwork during regular school hours; additional attempts are made to work out common training problems in the schools' workshops and classrooms and this further minimizes the need for homework.

The solving of instructional problems during regular class sessions can often effectively reinforce materials that were previously presented in lectures. This could be especially helpful to persons whose family background and formal schooling had not disciplined them to think independently.

In spite of the attempts to limit the hours of home study, a large percentage of all vocational schools do assign home work and certain courses demand as much study as collegiate programs.[33] There is, however, little doubt that some students miss the learning benefits which can be derived solely from individual problem-solving. Under a more favorable loan program many of these students might be inclined to borrow, work fewer hours and study more. Presumably the private schools could then adjust classroom presentations and home assignments.

Equalizing Educational Opportunities

Although a liberalized government loan program is an ideal way of enhancing equality of educational opportunity, the potential influences

[32] Ten percent of all students considered in Chapter 9 were receiving financial aid from Vocational Rehabilitation agencies or the Bureau of Indian Affairs; the extent to which these students may have also been represented in the group encountering severe financial difficulties is not known.

[33] More than 2/5 of the students in the electronics technology course at RCA Institutes study at least 16 hours weekly.

of a combined loan-grant program would be still greater for those persons who have lacked even the "hope" of attending a private vocational school. From a financial viewpoint, they include individuals who have exceptional family responsibilities or are members of low-income families. Educationally, they are the large number of public school dropouts and the multitude of persons who were provided with a mediocre "general education" that failed to prepare them for any vocation.[34]

It would be desirable on operational or administrative grounds for a government loan-grant program to be available to *all* persons seeking employment-related training in private vocational schools. There is, however, a more important reason for universalizing the program — namely, an impressive growth in social concern for and commitment to "free public education." A Presidential Commission made the following recommendation in 1966:

> A nationwide system of free public education through two years beyond high school (grade 14) should be established. The key institutions would be area technical schools and community colleges. The public vocational-technical schools would provide training in trade, technical and business occupations at the skilled worker level. The community colleges would provide liberal education as well as technical and semi-professional training. The two types of schools might in many instances be merged into a community education center offering both the theoretical foundation of trade, technical, and business occupations and the opportunity to "learn-by-doing" while pursuing liberal education or semi-professional training. Most of the students in both types of institutions would be high school graduates, though provision could also be made for former high school dropouts, college transfers, and adults. Remedial courses could be provided for those whose earlier preparation had been inadequate and for continuing education for adults with adequate educational foundations.[35]

Professor Arthur M. Ross, a former U. S. Commissioner of the Bureau of Labor Statistics, has noted certain weaknesses in most high schools and also recommended an increase in community vocational educational centers. He adds another alternative: " . . . the development of work-and-study combinations, in a wide variety of occupations, through collaboration between the educational authorities and the employers in an area."[36]

[34] As mentioned previously, many high school graduates are even unable to enter certain private vocational schools until they have completed an intensive preparatory course.

[35] Report of the National Commission on Technology, Automation, and Economic Progress, *Technology and the American Economy*, Vol. 1, February 1966, p. 46.

[36] Arthur M. Ross, "Rhetoric and Reality in Manpower," in *Manpower Tomorrow*, edited by Irving H. Siegel (New York: Augustus M. Kelley, 1967), p. 68.

As mentioned several times in this book, the private vocational schools' capabilities for motivating and training persons (including the disadvantaged) are usually neglected. This is partly attributable to the minor usage of these schools under many government training programs. It is possible that the schools will be recognized as an important training resource if the states decide to use them actively under the new provisions of the Vocational Education Act. The greater usage of proprietary schools could increase the alternatives of persons who desire to enroll in vocational training courses.

As shown in Chapter 2, equality of educational opportunity in the form of widely available general education or college preparatory programs in high school can be a myth and even a hoax. Many students simply lack either the interest or the ability to attend a college or even a junior college. Also, a community college, public technical institute, or area vocational school may be unavailable. Even if "free" schools are available, the courses that a prospective student wants may not be offered; or else, the course length and its contents may differ from his preferences.

In view of the free or heavily subsidized education that is accessible to a sizable and rapidly increasing number of students in universities, colleges and other public institutions, it would be equitable to improve the opportunities of students who choose to attend private vocational schools. The realistic and economically sound recognition and usage of the private schools (a proven training resource) could be a major means for expanding the laudable goal of equal educational opportunity.

A financial plan that is devised to aid students enrolling in private schools could be in the form of a partial loan-grant. One hypothetical plan was considered in Chapter 8. The non-borrowing students at RCA Institutes were asked: "Would you take out a loan if the government not *only* paid most of the interest but also one-half the principal on your loan?" Seventy percent of the students answered affirmatively. More than 4/5 of the students who would not borrow even under such very favorable terms said they depended on their parents or spouse for means of support or else they preferred to work rather than borrow; the remaining students relied on the G.I. Bill or various forms of state aid.

It is naturally not possible to know how representative the RCA Institutes' students are of all students attending private vocational schools. However, it is reasonable to assume that about 30 percent of all enrolled students will prefer *not* to take advantage of a partial loan-grant plan. Considerable doubt remains over the interest in such a plan on the part of students who have not been counseled about the schools or else have had inadequate funds to consider attending the schools. However, in order to be attractive and meaningful to prospective students (as well as many of the already enrolled students), the maximum amount of the loan-grant should be at least $2,000 annually.[37]

Even under a "universal" loan-grant plan, criteria would have to be formulated for the selection of participating students and conditions set for approved courses. Attendance ought to be limited to persons enrolling in vocational courses. The length of courses should probably have no minimum period. (A very intensive training program for heavy truck driving is only three weeks in duration, but the course charge to students is about $750.) The maximum period for an approved course could be set at two years, although most courses are 18 months or less in length. The maximum number of courses that a person would be allowed to enroll in is another important consideration. Under a Veterans Administration (VA) procedure, which might be adopted for this proposed plan, a qualified veteran may enroll in two different courses over a period of time. If a veteran decides to enroll in a third course, he must first undergo counseling and testing under VA auspices.

In addition to formulating criteria for the selection of students and setting conditions for approved courses, a list of acceptable participating schools would have to be made generally available. The schools accredited by agencies which the U. S. Commissioner of Education has recognized should naturally be able to participate in the loan-grant program. Since accreditation encompasses only a minority of all trade and technical schools, the Commissioner of Education has given special approval to the schools that are licensed and regulated by state authorities in about 15 states. As more schools apply for and receive accreditation, the Commissioner might decide to rely exclusively (or at least principally) upon the accrediting agencies in compiling a list of participating schools.[38]

Grants for Disadvantaged Students

Dr. Herbert E. Striner, of the Upjohn Institute, and others have proposed awarding government grants to a substantial number of

[37] The annual maximum under the National Vocational Student Loan Insurance Act of 1965 (merged with the Higher Education Act of 1965, as amended 1968) is set at $1,500. The federal government pays up to 7 percent annually on the unpaid balance of a loan while the student is in school and 3 percent interest on the unpaid balance during the repayment period.

[38] As noted before, the National Commission on Accrediting hopes to strengthen the accrediting process and improve the quality of the programs and instruction among the institutions of the associated accrediting agencies. If successful, this could further induce the U. S. Commissioner of Education to rely upon accrediting agencies.

disadvantaged persons enrolling in private vocational schools. Senator Hugh Scott, of Pennsylvania, and other Congressmen are strongly in favor of such a program, and Senator Scott plans to introduce a bill in the U. S. Senate that will provide for 100,000 "vocational education opportunity grants." Each grant would be for a maximum of two years' training and in the amount of $2,500 annually. The purpose of the Act will be:

> . . . to provide financial assistance for training in private vocational schools to persons 17 years of age or older who (1) are academically, socially, economically, or culturally disadvantaged and as a result thereof have not completed their secondary education or have not been able to obtain regular employment.

The passage of such a bill would be additional and encouraging recognition that equality of educational opportunity can also be pursued by expanding the scope of vocational education. It would also increase the utilization of a potentially significant resource for training the disadvantaged — the private vocational schools.

CHAPTER 11

Summary of Major Recommendations

In general, the major recommendations summarized here deal with the disadvantaged persons who could benefit from training offered by private vocational schools. However, the recommendations will also help persons who might tend to be ignored because, while they are not disadvantaged, they are either not motivated or not qualified to attend college. Suggestions that relate to the operations of the schools are intended to help students indirectly through qualitative improvements in training programs. The private schools, which are predominantly profit-seeking, happen to favor greater financial assistance for enrolled and prospective students rather than some form of direct subsidy to the schools.

1. State departments of education should encourage local school systems to undertake joint ventures with private vocational schools. Such programs, which are feasible under the Vocational Education Amendments of 1968, would secure more respect for vocational education and its students. The resultant broadening of educational and occupational choices would encourage and reward diversity; this ought to advance attainment of the goal of equal educational opportunity, whereas the unrealistic emphasis upon the college preparatory curriculum actually detours any movement toward the goal. Additionally, the availability of more alternatives for students in high school (and earlier for some students) could prove to be an important means for reducing the number of school dropouts, who would ultimately account for a substantial number of the disadvantaged.

2. Greater attention must be given to the needs, aspirations and capacities of public school students who fail to receive counseling in their homes or are miscounseled by their parents and others. There will have to be a sizable expansion in the number of counselors, and the special lag in vocational counseling must be remedied by educating more advisers on the great variety of occupational opportunities and the numerous means of preparing for them, including private vocational schools. Counselors should become familiar with all loans and grants that are or may become available for persons enrolling in vocational education courses. Individuals from low-income families

will often require special guidance with respect to the workings and usefulness of credit and the feasibility of borrowing to finance a vocational education.

3. The growing societal concern for maximizing educational attainments and occupational potentials could be shown by greatly liberalizing the student loan insurance program. The federal government should raise the annual loan limit to $2,000; and, in addition to paying most of the interest, the government should pay one-half of the principal on each loan.

The proposal for grants to 100,000 disadvantaged persons enrolling in private vocational schools deserves the serious consideration of Congress.

4. Except for vocational education curricula that are "traditional" or easily incorporated, the public schools should concentrate on improving general education for all students and always maintaining it at the highest possible level. This is important and challenging enough in view of the diverse capabilities of students and their different objectives, including: preparation for college; joint enrollment in a public school and a private vocational school; preparation for attendance at a vocational school after completion of high school.

5. The likelihood of higher achievements in general education and the implementation of the proposed loan-grant program should lead the private vocational schools to raise the levels of sophistication in many of their courses.

6. In view of the greater social roles which are contemplated for private vocational schools voluntary accreditation of the schools should be encouraged. The schools ought to be evaluated on the basis of their facility to motivate and to train persons of *different* abilities and interests and their success in preparing students for the occupational objectives clearly stated by the schools. State departments of education should have increased concern over the instruction provided in the private schools because of the likelihood of many students being enrolled jointly in a public school and a private vocational school. The state departments of education could perhaps devote most of their attention to the schools that are unaccredited, and also alternate, at two-and-one-half-year intervals, with private associations such as NATTS and UBSA, in the reevaluation of schools that have already been accredited.

The attempts in New York to elevate and maintain high standards of instruction and administration in the private schools could be emulated by other states. The Bureau of Occupational School Supervision has arranged, through an agreement with the New York State School of Industrial and Labor Relations at Cornell University, to provide a 30-clock-hour course in teaching methods for instructors in private vocational schools. The Bureau has also sponsored a course for directors in Private Trade School Administration. These courses could be required of each instructor and school administrator at three-year intervals.[1]

7. The job-oriented instruction and continuing sense of achievement that are produced by the private schools can themselves be the means for motivating many disadvantaged persons, as well as leading to direct employment. For many people, this is recommended over attempts to motivate first and train second.

For persons requiring extraordinary guidance, there could be government payments to the private vocational schools which would then subcontract for counseling services. The payments could naturally be contracted directly with those schools having professional counselors.

8. Private vocational schools have the capacity to expand their enrollments considerably, and they ought to be utilized in training various types of disadvantaged persons. For example, under Vocational Rehabilitation programs, many of the schools have accepted and successfully trained people who lacked a high school education and who in addition may have been physically and emotionally handicapped. In particular, many more unemployed and underemployed persons could be served under the Manpower Development and Training Act; and there should be more extensive direct government contracts with national associations of private schools which also have accrediting bodies that are recognized by the U. S. Commissioner of Education.

9. The flexible operations of the private schools should be more fully exploited. For example, frequent starting dates and the capability for enrolling persons on an individual basis (in contrast to enrolling a full class) can stem the sense of futility that overcomes many unemployed persons. Another adaptation — the mobile school — could be used in ghettos and, conversely, in sparsely populated areas.

10. The U. S. Office of Education is urged to publish a national directory of private vocational schools biennially and include such information as: minimum educational requirements for admission to the courses or programs in each of the schools; government programs in which the schools have participated; any accreditation earned by each school; and number of students enrolled.

[1] See New York, Bureau of Occupational School Supervision, *Annual Report,* July 1, 1966–June 30, 1967 (Albany), p. 2.

Survey Procedures for Postcard Questionnaire

Unless stated otherwise, the number of private vocational schools, enrolled students and training courses were estimated from responses to a short postcard questionnaire (see Exhibit 1) that was mailed in August 1967. The questionnaire was mailed to 2,606 schools in the following four occupational training categories: trade and technical, business, cosmetology and barbering. Schools' addresses were secured from lists provided by the National Association of Trade and Technical Schools, the United Business Schools Association and the Veterans Administration. The *members* of the National Association of Trade and Technical Schools were not sent a copy of the short questionnaire because they were requested to respond to a longer, more detailed questionnaire that is found in Appendix II.

A total of 955 schools responded to the first mailing of the postcard questionnaire. An additional 224 schools were excluded and this lowered the total number of potential respondents to 2,388. The principal reasons for excluding schools were as follows: correspondence or home study students comprised more than 50 percent of a school's enrollment; the admission requirement was higher than high school graduation; length of course exceeded two years; training was offered by a hospital and presumably only met the hospital's needs; the school was out of business or left no forwarding mail address; a school enrolled less than 10 students during the year 1966.[1] After the exclusion of these schools from the initial total, a response rate of 40 percent was recorded.[2]

Nearly 20 percent of the non-responding schools (244 in number) were then selected randomly for follow-up from geographically indexed cards representing the schools in three occupational groupings. The barber and cosmetology schools were combined into one

[1] Some of the schools with an enrollment of less than 10 students had probably been established during 1966, but only a few schools provided such information.

[2] The response rate by business schools was the highest of any group and this was largely due to the exceptional response by members of the United Business Schools Association. This factor was encouraging in view of the decision to send the long questionnaire shown in Appendix II only to members of the National Association of Trade and Technical Schools.

EXHIBIT 1

POSTCARD QUESTIONNAIRE[1]

CONFIDENTIAL
QUESTIONNAIRE: STUDY OF PRIVATE
OCCUPATIONAL-TRAINING SCHOOLS

1. About how many students attended courses in your school in 1966?
_____ students

2. About how many students were enrolled in correspondence courses?
_____ students

3. What is the minimum education for entering your school?
_____ years

4. List up to 5 of the major occupations for which your school trains:

5. Have any of your students trained under these Federal programs (check):
___a) Vocational Rehabilitation Act
___b) Manpower Development and Training Act
___c) Veterans Administration
___d) "Poverty" (OEO)
___e) Other (specify) _____

- -

TO: (NAME & ADDRESS OF SCHOOL)

(SIDE ONE)

[1] A similar questionnaire was signed by Richard A. Fulton, Exec. Dir. and General Counsel of the United Business Schools Association, and forwarded to the business schools.

NATIONAL ASSOCIATION OF TRADE AND TECHNICAL SCHOOLS
1601 — 18th Street, N.W., Washington, D. C. 20009

August 9, 1967

Gentlemen:

I am pleased, in my official capacity, to request your cooperation in answering the questions on the reverse side. Your answers (which will be kept *confidential*) are needed for the important first stage of a study of private occupational-training schools. Your cooperation will help our schools, our expanding number of students, our business clients, and government policy makers.

Please restaple this card after completion and return it within 10 days to Dr. Belitsky at the address shown below (send a copy of your catalog to the same address too).

Sincerely,
(s)
William Goddard
Executive Director

PERSON COMPLETING FORM

ADDRESS OF SCHOOL

DR. A. HARVEY BELITSKY
THE W. E. UPJOHN INSTITUTE
FOR EMPLOYMENT RESEARCH
1101 — 17th Street, N.W.
Washington, D.C. 20036

(SIDE TWO)

group because the schools are quite homogeneous and the absolute number of responses on the first mailout was large compared with the trade and technical group. One out of every 20 non-responding barber and cosmetology schools was selected. The trade and technical schools have great heterogeneity in course offerings and they had the largest absolute number of non-respondents; one out of every four schools was therefore selected from this group. The business schools were midway between the other two groups with regard to diversity of courses, and the absolute number of non-responses was smallest; one of every six non-responding schools was chosen.

The non-respondents who did complete the questionnaire during the second mailing totaled 44 percent, or a few percentage points higher than those schools responding to the initial mailout. Nine percent of the schools in both mailings were excluded for the variety of reasons given before.

Finally, a telephone follow-up of non-respondents to the second mailout was conducted after a goal of 13 schools was set; and by random selection the number of calls necessary to secure that total was made. When both mailouts and the telephone calls were combined, 1,067 schools out of 2,355 (or 45 percent) responded to the questionnaire.[3]

After the survey was undertaken, it became evident that a substantial number of schools were missing from either the lists of schools receiving the postcard questionnaire or the membership of the National Association of Trade and Technical Schools (NATTS) which received the long questionnaire shown in Appendix II. Whereas the Veterans Administration (VA) and NATTS lists of schools yielded nearly 1,150 trade and technical schools, a later list compiled by NATTS disclosed 2,300 schools. William Goddard, the Executive Director of NATTS, estimates that there are a minimum of 3,000 trade and technical schools.[4] Congressman Roman C. Pucinski, Chairman of the General Subcommittee on Education of the Committee on Education and Labor, estimates that the total number of *all* private vocational schools is 7,500, or about 400 more than the figure adopted in this study.

The 700 business schools that received the short questionnaire represented nearly 55 percent of all business schools according to a later estimate provided by the United Business Schools Association. The

---

[3] Some of the schools reporting enrollments of 1,000 or more students were requested to verify their figures by telephone.

[4] The VA list made available for this study contained a much smaller total number of schools because the names of some schools could not be identified; but, more important, the reports provided by individual states were apparently incomplete and some schools had no students who were being trained under the legislation when the states' reports were being prepared for the VA in Washington.

combined group of barber and cosmetology schools totaled 700 schools, but the associations for these two types of schools report the names of nearly 2,800 member schools. (Only the associations representing the barber and cosmetology schools were able to provide exact data on the number of schools.)

Despite the discrepancies in the total number of schools, it was decided to consider the questionnaire results "representative" because of the several sources — including the VA and private school associations — that were consulted in forming the surveyed "population." The results presented in Table 1 of Chapter 2 are not *statistically* significant.[5] However, the number of schools and enrolled students are considered reasonable estimates despite the sampling bias due to the large number of omitted schools discovered after completion of the survey.

[5] The test for difference of means did *not* disclose any significant differences between the average number of students enrolled in the schools responding to the first and second mailouts of the postcard questionnaire.

Questionnaire Directed to Members of the National Association of Trade and Technical Schools

Although this study was concerned with all private vocational schools having the capability for training disadvantaged persons, special emphasis was placed upon the trade and technical schools. Besides offering a great variety of occupational courses, about 45 percent of these schools were estimated to have at least one course which did not require graduation from high school for admission.

A long and detailed questionnaire (Exhibit 2) was pre-tested at several schools in the Washington, D.C. area and, as a result, the wording of some questions was clarified. The questionnaire was then sent to the 156 members of the National Association of Trade and Technical Schools (NATTS) on October 19, 1967. The Executive Director and officers of NATTS promised to encourage completion of the questionnaire by the member schools. This was done in several ways, including a covering letter with the questionnaire signed by the Executive Director, verbal announcements and a notice in the *NATTS News.*

Three weeks after the questionnaires were sent, a follow-up letter was mailed to the non-responding schools. Letters were also sent to those schools which failed to answer certain questions. Although some schools left a few questions unanswered, the total response was impressive: 128 schools, or 85 percent of the membership, completed the questionnaires.[1]

The answers to the 38 questions (often containing several parts) by each responding school provided important materials for nearly every chapter. The NATTS schools are identified throughout the book, particularly when the schools' responses are presented in tables.

[1] The original total of 156 schools was reduced by five when two schools went out of business and three branch schools resigned in protest over the failure of one of the schools to receive NATTS accreditation.
The membership of NATTS is now much larger.

EXHIBIT 2

LONG QUESTIONNAIRE

THE W. E. UPJOHN INSTITUTE FOR EMPLOYMENT RESEARCH
NATIONWIDE SURVEY OF
PRIVATE VOCATIONAL SCHOOLS

Name and Address of School

_____

_____

_____

Name and Title of Person Completing Questionnaire

_____

_____

INSTRUCTIONS FOR FILLING OUT QUESTIONNAIRE

1. *Definition of Words Used* — This questionnaire generally uses the word "course" to refer to the instruction in *major occupational areas* offered at your school. Many schools may actually use the word "program" instead of "course" in their catalogs. Therefore, please consider the word "course" *the same* as "program" for purposes of this questionnaire.

2. *Types of Courses and Students* — When answering, please do *not* take into account the following types of courses and students:

   a. Recreation and hobby courses and students enrolled in them.

   b. Correspondence courses and students enrolled in them.

   References to students, therefore, should be limited to those enrolled in occupational courses.

3. *Time Period* — When particular questions do not give a specific time period, please base your answer on your experience during the past 1 to 3 years.

4. *School Being Referred to* — Please limit your answers to the specific *school* to which this questionnaire has been mailed. The only exception should be your answer to Question 3.

   Use of Information Received — Your answers to all questions will be held CONFIDENTIAL. Reports based on the information received through these questionnaires will not identify any of the schools or persons cooperating in this research.

NATURE OF SCHOOL

1. When was your school established?
   a. _____ since 1965
   b. _____ between 1950–1964
   c. _____ between 1945–1949
   d. _____ between 1925–1944
   e. _____ between 1900–1924
   f. _____ before 1899

2. Is your school a:
   a. _____ single ownership
   b. _____ partnership
   c. _____ business corporation
   d. _____ nonprofit corporation approved by the Internal Revenue Service

3. If you own or franchise another private vocational school, please indicate where it (they) is (are) located. If you franchise any of the schools, please place an *F* next to those that are.

   _____ ,   _____
   _____ ,   _____
   _____ ,   _____
   _____ ,   _____
   _____ ,   _____
   _____ ,   _____
   _____ ,   _____

4. For how many years has your school been under its present ownership?
   a. _____ less than 2 years
   b. _____ 2–4 years
   c. _____ 5–9 years
   d. _____ 10–19 years
   e. _____ 20–29 years
   f. _____ more than 30 years

5. At present, what is your school's student *capacity* (the maximum number of students that *could* be enrolled)?

   PLEASE BE SURE TO PLACE A CHECK IN BOTH COLUMNS.

   1. *Number During Day (both morning and afternoon):*
      a. _____ less than 100
      b. _____ 100–199
      c. _____ 200–399
      d. _____ 400–749
      e. _____ 750–999
      f. _____ 1,000–2,499

g. _____ 2,500–3,999
h. _____ more than 4,000

2. *Number During Evening:*
    a. _____ less than 100
    b. _____ 100–199
    c. _____ 200–399
    d. _____ 400–749
    e. _____ 750–999
    f. _____ 1,000–2,499
    g. _____ more than 2,500

6. If you were able to, would you be interested in expanding the size of your school?

    a. yes_____
        no, because of:

    PLEASE CHECK ONE OR MORE OF THE FOLLOWING APPLICABLE EXPLANA-
    TION(S) AND CIRCLE THE MAJOR ONE.

    b. _____ management problems
    c. _____ shortage of instructors
    d. _____ competition of public schools
    e. _____ extra income not worth the effort
    f. _____ other (PLEASE DESCRIBE): _____
    _____
    _____
    _____

7. How many different occupational courses are offered at your school?

    CHECK ONE

    a. _____ 1 course
    b. _____ 2 courses
    c. _____ 3 courses
    d. _____ 4 courses
    e. _____ 5 courses
    f. _____ 6 courses
    g. _____ 7 courses
    h. _____ 8 courses
    i. _____ 9 courses
    j. _____ 10 courses
    k. _____ more than 10 different occupational courses
        PLEASE SPECIFY NUMBER_____ courses.

8. For each of the major occupational courses *offered at your school in 1966,* please provide the information requested below.

IF YOUR SCHOOL OFFERED MORE THAN 10 OCCUPATIONAL COURSES,
PLEASE LIMIT YOUR LIST TO THE 10 THAT USUALLY HAD THE LARGEST ENROLLMENT.

Major Occupational Course	Full-Tuition Cost to Student	Approx. No. of Students Enrolled in 1966	No. of Years Course Has Been Taught	Year When Course Was Last Revised
1.	$			19
2.	$			19
3.	$			19
4.	$			19
5.	$			19
6.	$			19
7.	$			19
8.	$			19
9.	$			19
10.	$			19

9(a). Is there a minimum educational requirement for admission to any of the major occupational courses you have listed in the preceding chart (question 8)?

    a. _____ No

                 Yes, there is a minimum educational requirement for major occupational course:

(PLEASE CHECK AS MANY AS APPLY)

b. _____ No. 1		g. _____ No. 6
c. _____ No. 2		h. _____ No. 7
d. _____ No. 3		i. _____ No. 8
e. _____ No. 4		j. _____ No. 9
f. _____ No. 5		k. _____ No. 10

9(b). What is this minimum educational requirement?

PLEASE SPECIFY THE REQUIREMENT ON THE CHART BELOW BY PLACING A CHECK OR CHECKS IN THE APPROPRIATE BOXES. TOTAL NUMBER OF CHECKS PLACED SHOULD CORRESPOND TO TOTAL GIVEN IN ANSWER TO QUESTION 9(a) ABOVE.

Major Occupational Course	1–6 years of schooling	7–9 years of schooling	10–11 years of schooling	12 (high school or high school equivalent)	12+ years of schooling
No. 1					
No. 2					
No. 3					
No. 4					
No. 5					
No. 6					
No. 7					
No. 8					
No. 9					
No. 10					

10. Is a prospective student required to pass an achievement or aptitude test in order to be admitted to any of the major occupational courses you have listed?

    a. _____ No

                 Yes, Course

(CHECK AS MANY AS APPLY)

b. _____ No. 1		g. _____ No. 6
c. _____ No. 2		h. _____ No. 7
d. _____ No. 3		i. _____ No. 8
e. _____ No. 4		j. _____ No. 9
f. _____ No. 5		k. _____ No. 10

11. If you have other entrance requirements for your major occupational courses, please specify below.

CHECK AS MANY AS APPLY

a. _____ age

b. _____ physical (PLEASE SPECIFY)

   _____

   _____

   _____

c. _____ other (PLEASE SPECIFY)

   _____

   _____

   _____

COURSES OFFERED

12. Approximately how many weeks during the year are occupational courses offered?

CHECK ONE

a. _____ 52

b. _____ 48–51

c. _____ 26–47

d. _____ less than 26

13. Do you provide instruction in basic skills (such as reading, writing, and arithmetic) that are usually considered below the sixth-grade level?

a. _____ Yes

b. _____ No

c. _____ Other. PLEASE DESCRIBE: _____

   _____

   _____

14. What is the typical student-teacher ratio in your school?

PLEASE CHECK ONE FOR BOTH CLASSROOM OR LECTURE AND SHOP, LABORATORY OR MACHINE PRACTICE.

No. of Students per Teacher	Classroom or Lecture	Shop, Laboratory or Machine Practice
10	_____	_____
10–14	_____	_____
15–19	_____	_____
20–24	_____	_____
25–29	_____	_____
30 or more	_____	_____

15. How do the instructors in your school let a student know how he is doing in a course?
    A. By placing check marks in column A, please indicate all of the procedures used in your school.
    B. In column B, please *rank* the procedures you have checked in order of their importance in your school. Start with the number 1 and continue until all the checked items have been accounted for.

	Column A	*Column B*
a. By giving him a letter or numerical grade (e.g., B+, C; 85%, 70%; etc.)	———	———
b. By giving him a general descriptive report (e.g., poor, fair, good, excellent; pass-fail; satisfactory-unsatisfactory; etc.	———	———
c. By reviewing his work in the classroom and/or shop	———	———
d. By holding individual instructor-student conferences	———	———
e. By using some other technique or techniques	———	———
PLEASE SPECIFY:		

16. Please indicate the division of a typical full-time student's time for a typical school day. Be certain to place checks under both the classroom and shop headings whenever applicable.

Division of a Student's Day	*Classroom or Lecture*	*Shop, Laboratory or Machine Practice*
a. 15% or less	———	———
b. 16–25%	———	———
c. 26–40%	———	———
d. 41–50%	———	———
e. more than 50%	———	———

17. Do you have a placement service for the students of your school?
    a. ——————— No
       Yes, the service is available to students:
    CHECK AS MANY AS APPLY
    b. ——————— while they are attending school
    c. ——————— upon graduation
    d. ——————— for life
    e. ——————— other (PLEASE DESCRIBE) ————————————

18. Do you secure follow-up information on your graduates' progress in employment?

    a. _____ No

    Yes:

Follow-up information is obtained:

CHECK AS MANY AS APPLY

    b. _____ within 6 months after graduation

    c. _____ one year after graduation

    d. _____ on an annual basis

    e. _____ other (PLEASE DESCRIBE) _____

_____

_____

19(a). Do you have a student loan program?

    a. _____ No

    b. _____ Yes

  (b). What percentage of your students receive the major part of their financing from your loan program?

    _____%

  (c). What percentage of your students receive the major part of their financing from bank loans?

    _____%

20. Do you have a deferred-payment system for students?

    a. _____ Yes

    b. _____ No

21. Has training for some of the students at your school ever been financed by Federal (or State) programs?

    a. _____ No

(CHECK AS MANY AS APPLY)

Yes, under the following Federal program:

    b. _____ Vocational Rehabilitation Programs for Disabled or Handicapped

    c. _____ Manpower Development and Training Programs

    d. _____ Veteran's Administration Programs — G. I. Bill, etc.

    e. _____ "Poverty" Program — Job Corps, Community Action, Neighborhood Youth Corps

    f. _____ Work Experience for Welfare Recipients Program of "Poverty" Program

    g. _____ Indian Affairs Training Program

    h. _____ Refugee Assistance

    i. _____ Immigration and Naturalization Service for Foreign Students

    j. _____ Federal Vocational Student Loan

    k. _____ Other (PLEASE SPECIFY) _____

_____

_____

NATURE OF STUDENT BODY

22. What percentage of students currently enrolled in your school attend day and/or night classes?
    a. _____% attending day classes
    b. _____% attending night classes

23. What percentage of students currently enrolled attend courses full-time or part-time?
    a. _____% attending full-time
    b. _____% attending part-time

24(a). How many students attended courses in your school *during 1966?*
    _____ students attended courses in 1966

  (b). How many of those who attended the courses actually completed them?
    _____ students actually completed courses in 1966

25. How many of the students who completed courses in 1966 were placed in jobs by your placement service?

   (PLEASE GIVE FIGURES FOR ACTUAL JOB PLACEMENTS RATHER THAN FOR JOB REFERRALS.)
    _____ number of students actually placed in jobs in 1966
    _____ school has no placement service

26. Approximately what percentage of the day and evening students who were expected to graduate from your school in 1966 did *not* actually do so?
    _____ approximate % of day students
    _____ approximate % of evening students

27(a). What has been the approximate average age of your students during the past 3 years?

   (PLEASE CHECK ONE SPACE IN BOTH COLUMNS.)

Average Age of Students	Day Students	Evening Students
a. 16–18	_____	_____
b. 19–21	_____	_____
c. 22–25	_____	_____
d. 26–30	_____	_____
e. 31–35	_____	_____
f. 36–40	_____	_____
g. over 40	_____	_____

  (b). During the past three years, what were the approximate ages of your youngest and oldest students?
    Youngest students were about _____ years old.
    Oldest students were about _____ years old.

28. Approximately what proportion of your day and evening students are male?

PLEASE PLACE ONE CHECK IN BOTH COLUMNS.

Percent of Male Students	Day Students	Evening Students
a. less than 10%		
b. 10%		
c. 20%		
d. 30%		
e. 40%		
f. 50%		
g. 60%		
h. 70%		
i. 80%		
j. 90%		
k. 100%		

29. Approximately what percent of your day and evening students have had the various amounts of schooling indicated on the chart below?

PLEASE FILL OUT EACH SPACE IN BOTH COLUMNS AND BE CERTAIN THAT YOUR FIGURES ADD UP TO 100%

Years of School	% Day Students	% Evening Students
1–6		
7–9		
10–11		
12 (high school or high school equivalent)		
12 or more		
Total	100%	100%

30. Approximately what percent of your students have permanent homes that are located within 50 miles of the school?

a. _____ none
b. _____ less than 10%
c. _____ more than 10%
d. _____ more than 25%
e. _____ more than 50%
f. _____ more than 75%

31. Approximately what percent of your students have their permanent homes in another state?

a. _____ none
b. _____ less than 10%
c. _____ more than 10%
d. _____ more than 25%
e. _____ more than 50%
f. _____ more than 75%

32. Please indicate the approximate number of foreign students (i.e., foreigners who reside in the United States only for purposes of study) enrolled in your school.

    _____ number of foreign students

33. Below are a number of reasons for giving vocational training in private schools rather than in public schools. On the basis of your own experience, which 5 would you consider most important?

    PLEASE DO NOT CHECK YOUR FIVE CHOICES. INSTEAD, PUT THE NUMBER 1 NEXT TO THE ITEM YOU CONSIDER FIRST MOST IMPORTANT, 2 NEXT TO THE SECOND MOST IMPORTANT, AND SO ON.

    a. _____ Private schools have more up-to-date equipment.
    b. _____ The training in the private schools is more practical.
    c. _____ Certain courses are not available in public schools.
    d. _____ Private vocational school graduates are more attractive to employers.
    e. _____ Private schools have frequent starting dates.
    f. _____ Course length in private schools is shorter.
    g. _____ The instructors in private schools are better prepared.
    h. _____ Private schools are more conveniently located.
    i. _____ Private schools have a placement service.
    j. _____ Other (PLEASE DESCRIBE) _____
    _____
    _____
    _____

34. Several incentives and ways of maintaining student interest are listed below. First, please *check* all those that apply in your school. Second, *circle* the two major ones.

    a. _____ demonstrations by outside visitors
    b. _____ visits by employers or their representatives
    c. _____ breakdown of course into small achievement units
    d. _____ public display of student projects
    e. _____ vocational counseling
    f. _____ visits to plants, offices
    g. _____ recreation activities
    h. _____ free passes to entertainment
    i. _____ other (PLEASE LIST) _____
    _____
    _____
    _____

35. Which *two* of the following do you consider the major reasons your *day students* do not complete their course?

    CHECK ONLY TWO ITEMS.

    a. _____ financial problems
    b. _____ lack of interest in the course

c. _____ lack of ability for the course
d. _____ generally low motivation
e. _____ securing a job before completing the course
f. _____ being drafted into military service
g. _____ personal or family problems
h. _____ other (PLEASE LIST) _____

_____

_____

_____

_____

36. Which *two* of the following do you consider the major reasons your *evening students* do not complete their course?

    CHECK ONLY TWO ITEMS.

a. _____ financial problems
b. _____ lack of interest in the course
c. _____ lack of ability for the course
d. _____ generally low motivation
e. _____ securing a job before completing the course
f. _____ being drafted into military service
g. _____ personal or family problems
h. _____ other (PLEASE LIST) _____

_____

_____

_____

_____

PROBLEMS, NEEDS, AND SUGGESTIONS

37. Please list your suggestions for changes in the operation of existing government programs, or ideas for new programs that you think would be of assistance to you or your students.

38. Please list your suggestions for creating desirable changes in the relationship between state education departments and private vocational schools.

Are you enclosing or forwarding copies of a few representative letters of appreciation (or "testimonials") from your former students or employers who have hired your students?

_____ Yes

_____ No

Are you forwarding a copy of your catalog or comparable publication?

_____ Yes

_____ No

Thank you for your cooperation.

(s)
A. Harvey Belitsky
Director, Study of Private Vocational Schools

Survey of Students at RCA Institutes

The questionnaire (Exhibit 3) was completed by the first-year students at RCA Institutes in New York City on February 16, 1968. The Dean of the school had previously notified the students that the questionnaire would require less than 15 minutes to answer during a regular class period.

Students in 38 classrooms completed the questionnaire.[1] As indicated in Chapter 8, some of the students undoubtedly misinterpreted the question dealing with hours of study. Also, less than five percent of the students did not answer the question dealing with race or else inserted irrelevant answers.

EXHIBIT 3

SURVEY OF PRIVATE SCHOOL STUDENTS

1. About how many hours do you have to study after school every week?
   a. 5 hours or less   _____
   b. 6–10 hours   _____
   c. 11–15 hours   _____
   d. 16–20 hours   _____
   e. 21–25 hours   _____
   f. Other (PLEASE INDICATE) _____
   _____
   _____

2. Do you have a job now?
   a. Yes   _____
   b. No   _____

3. If you have a job, how many hours do you work weekly?
   a. 10 or less hours   _____
   b. 11–19 hours   _____
   c. 20–25 hours   _____
   d. 26–35 hours   _____
   e. 36 hours or more   _____

[1] One class was on a field trip and was not included.

4. If you have a job, which of the following is the *main* reason why you are working while attending school?
   a. Pay for tuition & books   _____
   b. Pay for tuition & books & other expenses   _____
   c. I enjoy the work   _____
   d. The work is related to my course at school   _____
   e. Other (PLEASE EXPLAIN) _____
        _____
        _____

5. Please rank in 1, 2, 3 order, which of the following 3 are your *main* sources of financing your education:
   a. Employment   _____
   b. Savings   _____
   c. Parents   _____
   d. Scholarship   _____
   e. Loan   _____
   f. Other (PLEASE LIST) _____
        _____
        _____

6. Did your high school guidance counselor or a high school teacher ever tell you about the availability of loans for vocational students in such schools as RCA Institutes?
   a. Yes _____
   b. No _____

7. If there is a choice between working or borrowing money for all of your expenses while going to school, which would you prefer?
   a. Working   _____
   b. Borrowing   _____
   c. Combination of working and borrowing   _____
   d. Other (PLEASE INDICATE) _____
        _____
        _____

FOR STUDENTS WHO *ARE* BORROWERS

8. Did you increase the amount you were borrowing when the government raised the amount that could be borrowed to $1,000?
   a. Yes _____
   b. No _____
   c. I was already at the maximum _____

9. Would you increase the amount you are borrowing if the government again raised the amount that can be borrowed?
   a. Yes _____
   b. No _____

10. If yes, would you then stop working or try to reduce the number of hours you are working?

    a. Yes   _____

    b. No   _____

FOR STUDENTS WHO *ARE NOT* BORROWERS

11. Which one of the following reasons best explains why you did not apply for a government backed loan?

    a. I would rather work and pay now than borrow and pay later. _____

    b. I could not get a loan from the bank(s) that I went to. _____

    c. I could not be sure that I would be able to pay back a loan. _____

    d. I have other sources of income. _____

    e. I may have to enter the military service after graduation from school. _____

    f. I didn't know I might qualify for a loan. _____

    g. Other (PLEASE EXPLAIN) _____

    _____

    _____

12. Would you take out a loan if the government not *only* paid most of the interest but also one-half the principal on your loan?

    a. Yes   _____

    b. No   _____

The following statements say certain things about school, work, or life in general. Circle the number to the right of each statement that shows how much you agree or disagree. For example, if you circle "1" it means that you agree completely; while "5" means that you disagree completely. Please *circle one* number for *each* statement. There are, of course, no right or wrong answers.

	Strongly Agree	Agree Somewhat	Not Sure	Disagree Somewhat	Strongly Disagree
13. Most work is dull and boring and I wouldn't do it if I didn't need the money.	1	2	3	4	5
14. During my spare time I almost always have something to do which I enjoy.	1	2	3	4	5
15. What you learn in school is of little value in meeting the problems of real life.	1	2	3	4	5
16. In my life so far I have almost always been lucky.	1	2	3	4	5
17. I feel that if I try hard enough, I have a good chance of succeeding at whatever I want to do.	1	2	3	4	5

	Strongly Agree	Agree Somewhat	Not Sure	Disagree Somewhat	Strongly Disagree
18. The way things are now, I might as well buy what I want today and let tomorrow take care of itself.	1	2	3	4	5
19. I feel I am as capable and smart as most other people.	1	2	3	4	5
20. I feel that it is best not to expect too much out of life and be content with what comes my way.	1	2	3	4	5
21. I have found that most teachers have it in for me and give me a hard time.	1	2	3	4	5
22. It pays off if you work hard on a job.	1	2	3	4	5
23. A high school education is worth all the time and effort it requires.	1	2	3	4	5
24. Most people look out for themselves and are not interested in helping others.	1	2	3	4	5

PLEASE INDICATE YOUR:

Age _____ Years old

Race _____

Home Address (state only) _____

Survey Procedures for Specialty Oriented Student Research Data

The impressions and observations presented in Chapter 9 are limited to students who attended the private trade schools participating in the Specialty Oriented Student Research (SOS) Program of the University of Iowa. The schools are not necessarily representative of all private trade schools because they either volunteered to participate in the SOS research program or they were recommended to Dr. Kenneth B. Hoyt and his University associates by high school counselors.

Besides the absence of random selection, students completed questionnaires at different levels of personal progress in either their schooling or job experiences. This must be considered along with the geographical dispersion of the schools. In a sense, possible time and regional differences were "collapsed" in order to secure a maximum number of students.

Students completed questionnaires both while they were enrolled in school and six months and one and one-half years following their departure from school; the period covered 1963–1966.

The first questionnaire dealt with some of the characteristics and experiences of the students. One year later, the personnel conducting the SOS Research Program secured the names of those students who had been out of school for six months and they were the only ones sent a questionnaire in the first follow-up; this group represented 70 percent of the students completing the first questionnaire.

The second follow-up questionnaire was completed two years after the first questionnaire. Only those persons who had been out of school for one and one-half years received the questionnaire; as in the case of the first follow-up, only about 70 percent of the students met the qualification.

An additional caution must be raised with respect to student non-response rate. In general, much less than five percent of the students failed to answer questions dealing with their periods of schooling and first full-time job;[1] but the rate was much higher for questions concerned

[1] These periods accounted for more than 60 percent of the questions.

with succeeding employment experiences. In each follow-up therefore a substantial statistical bias was evident, and the data must be interpreted as representing the views of the *responding* students.

Data of the SOS Research Program were utilized to determine what differences, if any, were present in the experiences and attainments of high school graduates and school dropouts while they were students in private trade schools and later when they were employed full-time.

As explained in Chapter 9, formal education level (fel), divided into three categories, was the major way of distinguishing the students for analysis. The chi-square tested for association between the fel of students and more than 30 of their responses or impressions regarding the private vocational schools they were attending and the full-time jobs they secured after leaving school.

Index